Android Studio 2 Essentials

Second Edition

A fast-paced guide to get you up and running with
Android application development using Android Studio 2

Belén Cruz Zapata

BIRMINGHAM - MUMBAI

Android Studio 2 Essentials
Second Edition

First published: January 2015

Second edition: June 2016

Production reference: 1170616

Published by Packt Publishing Ltd.
Livery Place
35 Livery Street
Birmingham B3 2PB, UK.

ISBN 978-1-78646-795-9

www.packtpub.com

Credits

Author
Belén Cruz Zapata

Reviewer
Antonio Hernández Niñirola

Commissioning Editor
Wilson D'souza

Acquisition Editor
Larissa Pinto

Content Development Editor
Sweta Basu

Technical Editor
Prajakta Mhatre

Copy Editor
Charlotte Carneiro

Project Coordinator
Bijal Patel

Proofreader
Safis Editing

Indexer
Mariammal Chettiyar

Production Coordinator
Aparna Bhagat

Cover Work
Aparna Bhagat

About the Author

Belén Cruz Zapata received her engineer's degree in computer science from the University of Murcia in Spain, specializing in software technologies, and intelligent and knowledge technologies. She earned an MSc in computer science and is now working on her PhD in the Software Engineering Research Group from the University of Murcia.

During the 2013/2014 academic year, Belén collaborated with the Université Mohammed V-Soussi, in Rabat, Morocco. Her research is focused on usability applied to mobile health (mHealth) applications.

Belén is currently working as a mobile developer for Android and iOS in the San Francisco Bay area. She is also the author of the book: *Testing and Securing Android Studio Applications*, *Packt Publishing*.

To follow her projects, you can visit her personal webpage at `http://www.belencruz.com` and you can follow her on Twitter: `@belen_cz`.

I would like to thank Packt Publishing for offering me the opportunity to write this book. I would particularly like to thank Larissa Pinto and Sweta Basu for their valuable help.

Each book represents a different period of my life, and this time, I would like to thank all my JCF-related friends here in San Francisco, for making it easier to live far from home. I would also like to thank my lifelong friends, my family, and my significant other, for being always with me.

About the Reviewer

Antonio Hernández Niñirola is a European PhD candidate in software engineering, which is the last step of the doctorate program. He did his BSc in computer science, and has a masters degree from the University of Murcia in Spain.

He has been in San Francisco since May 2015, working as a part of the Android Development Team at Yelp.

Antonio has collaborated with Packt Publishing as both author and reviewer several times. If you want to learn more advanced techniques on testing and security for Android, check out his book *Testing and Securing Android Studio Applications*. If you are new to Android development, check out these other books he has reviewed for Packt Publishing: *Android Studio Application Development* and *Android Studio Essentials* (first and second edition). If you would like to develop games for Android, check out *Mastering Android Game Development*.

For more information about him, visit his personal website (`http://www.ninirola.es`). Feel free to reach out on Twitter to `@hdezninirola` if you have any questions concerning Android or software engineering in general.

www.PacktPub.com

eBooks, discount offers, and more

Did you know that Packt offers eBook versions of every book published, with PDF and ePub files available? You can upgrade to the eBook version at www.PacktPub.com and as a print book customer, you are entitled to a discount on the eBook copy. Get in touch with us at customercare@packtpub.com for more details.

At www.PacktPub.com, you can also read a collection of free technical articles, sign up for a range of free newsletters and receive exclusive discounts and offers on Packt books and eBooks.

https://www2.packtpub.com/books/subscription/packtlib

Do you need instant solutions to your IT questions? PacktLib is Packt's online digital book library. Here, you can search, access, and read Packt's entire library of books.

Why subscribe?

- Fully searchable across every book published by Packt
- Copy and paste, print, and bookmark content
- On demand and accessible via a web browser

Table of Contents

Preface

Mobile applications have had a huge increase in popularity in the last few years and interest is still growing among users. Mobile operating systems are available not only for smart phones, but tablets as well, therefore increasing the possible market share for these applications.

Android has characteristics that make it pleasant for developers such as open source and having a high level of community, driven development. Android has always been in competition with iOS (the Apple mobile system) in everything and with XCode, iOS presented itself as a more centralized development environment. The new Android Studio IDE makes this centralization finally available for Android developers and makes this tool indispensable for a good Android developer.

This book about Android Studio shows users how to develop and build Android applications with this new IDE. It is not only a getting started book, but also a guide for advanced developers on building their applications faster and more productively. This book will follow a tutorial approach from the basic features to the steps to build for release, including practical examples.

What this book covers

Chapter 1, *Installing and Configuring Android Studio*, describes the installation and basic configuration of Android Studio.

Chapter 2, *Starting a Project*, shows how to create a new project and the type of activities we can select.

Chapter 3, *Navigating a Project*, explores the basic structure of a project in Android Studio.

Chapter 4, Using the Code Editor, exposes the basic features of the code editor in order to get the best out of it.

Chapter 5, Creating User Interfaces, focuses on the creation of user interfaces, using both the graphical view and the text-based view.

Chapter 6, Tools, exposes some additional tools, such as the Android SDK tools, Javadoc, and the version control integration.

Chapter 7, Google Play Services, introduces the current existing Google Play Services and how to integrate them into a project in Android Studio.

Chapter 8, Debugging, shows in detail how to debug an application in Android Studio and the provided information when debugging.

Chapter 9, Preparing for Release, describes how to prepare your application for release.

Appendix, Getting Help, introduces how to get help using Android Studio and provides a list of online sites to learn more about the topics covered in this book.

What you need for this book

For this book, you need a computer with a Windows, Mac OS, or Linux system. You will also need to have Java installed in your system.

Who this book is for

This book is not only a getting started book, but also a guide for advanced developers who have not used Android Studio to build their Android apps before. This book is great for developers who want to learn the key features of Android Studio and for developers who want to create their first app. It's assumed that you are familiar with the object-oriented programming paradigm and the Java programming language. It is also recommended that you understand the main characteristics of the Android mobile system.

Conventions

In this book, you will find a number of text styles that distinguish between different kinds of information. Here are some examples of these styles and an explanation of their meaning.

Code words in text, database table names, folder names, filenames, file extensions, pathnames, dummy URLs, user input, and Twitter handles are shown as follows: "The AppData directory is usually a hidden directory."

A block of code is set as follows:

```
package ${PACKAGE_NAME};

import android.app.Activity;
import android.os.Bundle;

#parse("File Header.java")
public class ${NAME} extends Activity {
    @Override
    public void onCreate(Bundle savedInstanceState) {
        super.onCreate(savedInstanceState);
    }
}
```

When we wish to draw your attention to a particular part of a code block, the relevant lines or items are set in bold:

```
if (savedInstanceState != null) {

}
```

New terms and **important words** are shown in bold. Words that you see on the screen, for example, in menus or dialog boxes, appear in the text like this: "You can also open it by clicking on the **Project** button on the left edge of the screen."

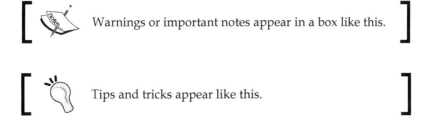

Warnings or important notes appear in a box like this.

Tips and tricks appear like this.

Reader feedback

Feedback from our readers is always welcome. Let us know what you think about this book—what you liked or disliked. Reader feedback is important for us as it helps us develop titles that you will really get the most out of.

To send us general feedback, simply e-mail `feedback@packtpub.com`, and mention the book's title in the subject of your message.

If there is a topic that you have expertise in and you are interested in either writing or contributing to a book, see our author guide at `www.packtpub.com/authors`.

Customer support

Now that you are the proud owner of a Packt book, we have a number of things to help you to get the most from your purchase.

Downloading the example code

You can download the example code files for this book from your account at `http://www.packtpub.com`. If you purchased this book elsewhere, you can visit `http://www.packtpub.com/support` and register to have the files e-mailed directly to you.

You can download the code files by following these steps:

1. Log in or register to our website using your e-mail address and password.
2. Hover the mouse pointer on the **SUPPORT** tab at the top.
3. Click on **Code Downloads & Errata**.
4. Enter the name of the book in the **Search** box.
5. Select the book for which you're looking to download the code files.
6. Choose from the drop-down menu where you purchased this book from.
7. Click on **Code Download**.

You can also download the code files by clicking on the **Code Files** button on the book's webpage at the Packt Publishing website. This page can be accessed by entering the book's name in the **Search** box. Please note that you need to be logged into your Packt account.

Once the file is downloaded, please make sure that you unzip or extract the folder using the latest version of:

- WinRAR / 7-Zip for Windows
- Zipeg / iZip / UnRarX for Mac
- 7-Zip / PeaZip for Linux

The code bundle for the book is also hosted on GitHub at `https://github.com/PacktPublishing/Android_Studio_2_Essentials_Second_Edition_Code`. We also have other code bundles from our rich catalog of books and videos available at `https://github.com/PacktPublishing/`. Check them out!

Downloading the color images of this book

We also provide you with a PDF file that has color images of the screenshots/diagrams used in this book. The color images will help you better understand the changes in the output. You can download this file from `https://www.packtpub.com/sites/default/files/downloads/AndroidStudio2EssentialsSecondEdition_ColorImages.pdf`.

Errata

Although we have taken every care to ensure the accuracy of our content, mistakes do happen. If you find a mistake in one of our books — maybe a mistake in the text or the code — we would be grateful if you could report this to us. By doing so, you can save other readers from frustration and help us improve subsequent versions of this book. If you find any errata, please report them by visiting `http://www.packtpub.com/submit-errata`, selecting your book, clicking on the **Errata Submission Form** link, and entering the details of your errata. Once your errata are verified, your submission will be accepted and the errata will be uploaded to our website or added to any list of existing errata under the Errata section of that title.

To view the previously submitted errata, go to `https://www.packtpub.com/books/content/support` and enter the name of the book in the search field. The required information will appear under the **Errata** section.

Piracy

Piracy of copyrighted material on the Internet is an ongoing problem across all media. At Packt, we take the protection of our copyright and licenses very seriously. If you come across any illegal copies of our works in any form on the Internet, please provide us with the location address or website name immediately so that we can pursue a remedy.

Please contact us at copyright@packtpub.com with a link to the suspected pirated material.

We appreciate your help in protecting our authors and our ability to bring you valuable content.

Questions

If you have a problem with any aspect of this book, you can contact us at questions@packtpub.com, and we will do our best to address the problem.

1
Installing and Configuring Android Studio

The new and official Google **Integrated Development Environment** (IDE) Android Studio 2.0 with all its varied features is ready to be explored. How would you like to make your own Android applications and make these applications available to other users on Google Play Store? Can you do this easily? How can you achieve this?

This chapter will show you how to prepare your new Android Studio installation and help you take your first steps in the new environment. We will begin by preparing the system for the installation and downloading the required files. We will see the welcome screen that prompts when running Android Studio for the first time, and we'll configure the **Android Software Development Kit** (**SDK**) properly so that you have everything ready to create your first application.

These are the topics we'll be covering in this chapter:

- Installing Android Studio
- Running Android Studio for the first time
- Configuring the Android SDK

Preparing for installation

A prerequisite to start working with Android Studio is to have Java installed on your system. The system must also be able to find the Java installation. This can be achieved by installing the **Java Development Kit** (**JDK**) on your system and then setting an environment variable named JAVA_HOME, which points to the JDK folder in your system. Check this environment variable to avoid issues during the installation of Android Studio.

Downloading Android Studio

The Android Studio package can be downloaded from the Android developer tools web page at `http://developer.android.com/sdk/index.html` by clicking on the download button, as is shown in the next screenshot. This package will be an EXE file for Windows systems, a DMG file for Mac OS X systems, or a TGZ file for Linux systems:

Installing Android Studio

In Windows, launch the EXE file. The default installation directory is `\Users\<your_user_name>\AppData\Local\Android\android-studio`. The `AppData` directory is usually a hidden directory.

In Mac OS X, open the DMG file and drop Android Studio into your `Applications` folder. The default installation directory is `/Applications/Android\ Studio.app`.

In Linux systems, unzip the TGZ file and execute the `studio.sh` script located at the `android-studio/bin/` directory.

If you have any problem in the installation process or in the following steps, you can get help about it and the known issues by checking *Appendix*, *Getting Help*.

Running Android Studio for the first time

Execute Android Studio and wait until it loads completely. This may take a few minutes the first time. The first time you execute Android Studio, you will be prompted by a welcome screen. As shown in the following screenshot, the welcome screen provides options to start a new project, open a project, import a project, or even perform more advanced actions, such as checking out a project from a version control system or modifying the configuration options:

Let's have a look at the various options available on the welcome screen:

- **Start a new Android Studio project**: This creates a new Android project from scratch

- **Open an existing Android Studio project**: This opens an existing project

- **Check out project from Version Control**: This creates a new project by importing existing sources from a version control system

- **Import project (Eclipse ADT, Gradle, etc.)**: This creates a new project by importing existing sources from your system

- **Import an Android code sample**: This imports a project containing the official Google code samples from GitHub (`https://github.com/googlesamples`)

The welcome screen, in addition to the main actions, also contains a configuration menu and a help menu, as described in the following:

- **Configure**: This opens the configuration menu. The configuration menu has the following options:
  - ○ **SDK Manager**: This opens the Android SDK tool that will be explained in *Chapter 6, Tools*.
  - ○ **Preferences**: This opens the Android Studio preferences.
  - ○ **Plugins**: This opens the plugins manager for Android Studio.
  - ○ **Import Settings**: This imports the settings from a file (.jar).
  - ○ **Export Settings**: This exports the settings to a file (.jar).
  - ○ **Settings Repository**: This allows you to enter the URL of an external code repository.
  - ○ **Check for Update**: This checks if there is an Android Studio update available.
  - ○ **Project Defaults**: This opens the project default settings menu.
  - ○ **Settings**: This opens the template project settings. These settings are also reachable through the Android Studio settings (**Configure | Settings**).
  - ○ **Project Structure**: This opens the project and platform settings.
  - ○ **Run Configurations**: This opens the run and debug settings.

- **Get Help**: This opens the help menu:
  - ○ **Help Topics**: This opens the Android Studio help, an online version
  - ○ **Tips of the Day**: This opens a dialog with the tip of the day
  - ○ **Default Keymap Reference**: This opens an online PDF containing the default keymap
  - ○ **Plugin Development**: This opens a JetBrains website containing information for plugin developers

Configuring the Android SDK

The essential feature that has to be correctly configured is the Android SDK. Although, Android Studio automatically installs the latest Android SDK available, so you should already have everything you need to create your first application. It is important to check it and learn how we can change it.

In the Android Studio welcome screen, navigate to **Configure | Project Defaults | Project Structure**. In SDK Location, you should have a selected **Android SDK location** as shown in the following screenshot. This selected SDK location is the default that will be used in our Android projects; however, we can change it later for specific projects that require special settings.

If you do not have an Android SDK configured in Android Studio, then we have to add it manually.

To accomplish this task, click on the ellipsis (...) button to add an Android SDK and then select the home directory for the SDK. Check whether you have it in your system by navigating to your Android Studio installation directory. You should find a folder named sdk, which contains the Android SDK and its tools. The Android Studio installation directory may be in a hidden folder; so, click on the button highlighted in the following screenshot to **Show Hidden Files and Directories**:

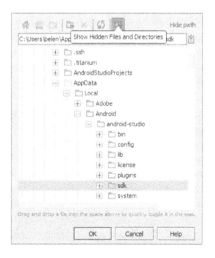

If you wish to use another Android SDK location that is different from the one included with Android Studio, select this instead. For example, if you previously used the **Android Development Tools (ADT)** plugin for Eclipse, you already have an Android SDK installation in your system.

Summary

We have successfully prepared the system for Android Studio and installed our Android Studio instance. We ran Android Studio for the first time, and now we know the options available in the welcome screen. You have also learned how to configure our Android SDK and to install it manually, in case you wish to use a different version. Completing these tasks will leave your system with Android Studio running and configured to create your first project.

In the next chapter, you will learn about the concept of a project and how it includes everything the application requires, from classes to libraries. We will create our first project and discuss the different kinds of activities available in the wizard.

2
Starting a Project

Now that you have installed Android Studio, the next thing to do is to get familiar with its features. You need to understand the necessary fields and form factors when creating a project. Also, you may need to choose the activity type to create the main activity. How can you achieve this using Android Studio?

In this chapter, we will discuss how to create a new project with the basic content that is needed to start out. We will use the Android Studio wizard to create the project and go through the project configuration fields. We will also select one of the different kinds of activities available in the wizard as our main activity.

These are the topics we'll be covering in this chapter:

- Creating a new project
- Selecting the parameters
- Choosing your main activity from different types of activities
- Customizing your main activity

Creating a new project

To create a new project, click on the **Start a new Android Studio project** option from the welcome screen. If you are not in the welcome screen, then navigate to **File | New Project**. This opens the **New Project** wizard, as shown in the following screenshot:

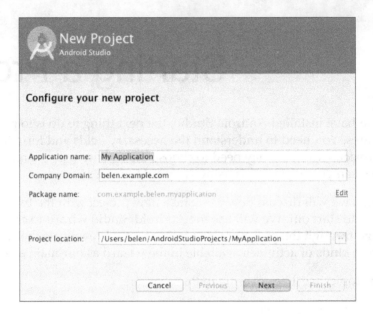

Configuring the project

The fields that will be shown on the **New Project** wizard are as follows:

- **Application name**: This is the name shown in Google Play and the name that users see.

- **Company Domain**: This is the company or domain name that is used to create the package name of your application.

- **Package name**: This is the unique identifier of your application, usually in the `com.company_name.app_name` or `reverse_company_domain.app_name` form. This form reduces the risk of name conflicts with other applications. A default package name is proposed, based on the **Company Domain** and **Application name** fields. You can change the package name by clicking on **Edit**.

- **Project location**: This is the directory in your system in which the project is saved.

Complete the information for your project and click on the **Next** button. This will take you to the second screen. This screen allows you to select your platform and the minimum SDK your project will support on different devices.

Selecting the form factors

Because of the way Android has expanded to different types of devices, you may want to select one or more kinds of platforms and devices to be included in your project. For each type of device, you can select a different minimum SDK. The devices Android supports are as follows:

- **Phone and Tablet**: These are standard Android platforms used to create an application for phones and/or tablets.

- **Wear**: This is an Android Wear platform used to design applications for wearable devices such as smartwatches.

- **TV**: This is an Android TV platform used to design applications for big screens, such as those of television sets.

- **Android Auto**: This is an extension to the Android platform to enable your app to work in cars. There is no platform selector for Android Auto because it depends on a standard **Phone and Tablet** project. Your app needs to target Android 5.0 or higher to support Android Auto.

- **Glass**: This is an Android Glass platform used to design applications for Google Glass devices.

Once you've decided on your devices, you can choose the minimum SDK supported by your application. Devices with an older SDK will not be able to install your application. Try to reach a balance between supported devices and available features. If your application does not require a specific feature published in the newest SDKs, then you can select an older **Application Programming Interface (API)**. The last dashboards published by Google about platform distribution show that 97.3 percent of the devices use Android 4.0.3 Ice Cream Sandwich or a later version. If you select Android 2.3.3 Gingerbread, then the percentage rises to almost 100 percent. You can check out these values by clicking on the **Help me choose** link. The official Android dashboards are also available at `http://developer.android.com/about/dashboards/index.html`.

To include any of the platforms and SDKs in your project, you need to have them installed in your system. The usual way to install a new platform is using a tool known as Android SDK Manager, which will be explained in *Chapter 6, Tools*. You don't have to use the manager now since the wizard to create a new project does all the work for you.

Check the **Phone** and **Tablet** option and select API 16 as the minimum SDK. After that, click on **Next**. The required components will be installed if necessary. If this is your case, click on **Next** again once the installation is completed. This will take you to the next screen where you can select the activity type.

Choosing the activity type

Activities are the components associated with the screens with which users interact in an application. The logic of an activity is implemented in a Java class with the name of the activity, which is created inside the source folder of your project. Android applications usually have multiple screens and are usually based on multiple activities. All the activities of an application have to be declared in the AndroidManifest.xml file. It is mandatory in any Android application since it describes essential information about the application. In *Chapter 3*, *Navigating a Project*, you will learn about the project structure and the AndroidManifest.xml file.

When an application is launched, it shows the main screen of the application. This step of the **New Project** wizard creates the main activity of your application, which is the main entry point of your application. You can indicate the type of activity you want to create as the main activity of your application. You can complete the creation of a new project without adding an activity, but you will need to add a main activity when you are finished creating your project. You can also change your main activity later in your project by modifying the AndroidManifest.xml file. You will be able to add new activities to complete your application once your project is created. To create new activities you can use this same wizard step in the menu by navigating to **File | New | Activity | Gallery**.

Several types of activities that can be selected are as follows:

- **Basic Activity**: This template creates an activity with an action bar and a floating action button. The action bar includes a title and an options menu. Action bars can provide navigation modes and user actions. You can read more about action bars at http://developer.android.com/guide/topics/ui/actionbar.html.

> You can read more about floating action buttons at https://www.google.com/design/spec/components/buttons-floating-action-button.html.

The following screenshot shows **Basic Activity**:

If you select this template, Android Studio will create a project with two layout files (`activity_main.xml` and `content_main.xml`) and the main activity class. The main layout (`activity_main.xml`) declares the action bar and the floating action button, and includes the content layout (`content_main.xml`) by adding the following XML declaration:

```
<include layout="@layout/content_main" />
```

- **Empty Activity**: This creates a blank activity. Here is a screenshot showing **Empty Activity**:

- **Fullscreen Activity**: This template hides the system's user interface (such as the notification bar) in a fullscreen view. By default, the fullscreen mode is alternated with an action bar that shows up when the user touches the device screen. **Fullscreen Activity** is shown in the following screenshot:

If you select this template, Android Studio will create a project with a main activity and its main layout. The main activity contains all the logic to handle the fullscreen mode. For example, you will notice two helper methods that hide and show the action bar:

```
private void hide() {
    ...
}

private void show() {
    ...
}
```

And you will notice the constant variables to configure whether the bar should hide automatically after a delay and the time of that delay:

```
/**
 * Whether or not the system UI should be auto-hidden after
 * {@link #AUTO_HIDE_DELAY_MILLIS} milliseconds.
 */
private static final boolean AUTO_HIDE = true;
/**
 * If {@link #AUTO_HIDE} is set, the number of milliseconds to
wait after
 * user interaction before hiding the system UI.
 */
private static final int AUTO_HIDE_DELAY_MILLIS = 3000;
```

- **Google AdMob Ads Activity**: This template creates an activity with a contained **AdMob Ad**. The purpose of this template is to display ads that allow monetizing your app. Here is a screenshot showing **Google AdMob Ads Activity**:

Google AdMob Ads Activity

If you select this template, Android Studio will create a project with a main activity and its main layout. The main activity contains all the logic to create (newInterstitialAd method), load (loadInterstitial method), and show (showInterstital method) ads, which are saved in an InterstitialAd object.

• **Google Maps Activity**: This template creates a new activity with a Google map in a fragment. A fragment is a portion of user interface in an activity. Fragments can be reused in multiple activities, and multiple fragments can be combined in a single activity. See more about fragments at https:// developer.android.com/guide/components/fragments.html. It is shown in the next screenshot:

If you select this template, Android Studio will create a project with a main activity and a layout containing the following map fragment:

```
<fragment xmlns:android="http://schemas.android.com/apk/res/
android"
xmlns:map="http://schemas.android.com/apk/res-auto"
xmlns:tools="http://schemas.android.com/tools"
android:id="@+id/map"
android:name="com.google.android.gms.maps.SupportMapFragment"
android:layout_width="match_parent"
android:layout_height="match_parent"
tools:context="com.example.mapstest.MapsActivity" />
```

- **Login Activity**: This template creates a view as a login screen, allowing the users to log in or register with e-mail and password.

If you select this template, Android Studio will create a project with a main activity and its layout. The main layout contains: a `ProgressBar` to show the login progress, an `AutoCompleteTextView` for the user's e-mail, an `EditText` for the user's password, and a `Button` to sign in.

The main activity includes code to autocomplete the e-mail, code to change the focus from one field to another, an `AsyncTask` class to perform the login in background, and code to show the progress of the login.

- **Master/Detail Flow**: This template splits the screen into two sections: a left-hand-side menu and the details of the selected item on the right-hand side. On a smaller screen, just one section is displayed, but on a bigger screen, both sections are displayed at the same time.

If you select this template, Android Studio will create a project with two activities: the list activity and the detail activity. The project also contains the two layouts for both activities: the list layout and the detail layout. There are some additional classes, such as a detail fragment and layouts to create the master list.

- **Navigation Drawer Activity**: This template creates a new activity with a navigation drawer. It displays the main navigation options in a panel that is brought onto the screen from a left-hand-side panel. You can read more about navigation drawers at `https://developer.android.com/design/patterns/navigation-drawer.html`.

Navigation Drawer Activity

This template contains a main activity that implements the `NavigationView.OnNavigationItemSelectedListener` interface. This listener allows the activity to receive an event when the user selects an option from the drawer menu. Events are received in the `onNavigationItemSelected` method implemented by the main activity:

```
@Override
public boolean onNavigationItemSelected(MenuItem item) {
    ...
}
```

The main layout is `DrawerLayout`, which contains a `NavigationView` object. Extra layouts are also created in the project for the main content, the main top bar, and the drawer header views.

- **Scrolling Activity**: This template creates an activity that scrolls vertically.

Scrolling Activity

This template contains a main activity and a main layout. The main layout has a `Toolbar` and includes the scroll content layout:

```
<include layout=""@layout/content_scrolling"" />
```

The content layout is `NestedScrollView`.

- **Settings Activity**: This creates a preferences activity with a list of settings:

This template has two activities: the main activity and the preferences activity. The preferences activity extends the `PreferenceActivity` class and overrides the methods to build the preferences screen. The preferences content is configured using the XML files that define the `PreferenceScreen` components.

- **Tabbed Activity**: This creates a blank activity with an action bar similar to **Basic Activity**, but it also includes a navigational element. The navigational element can be a tabbed user interface (fixed or scrollable tabs), a horizontal swipe, or a spinner menu. The project content generated by Android Studio depends on the navigational element selected.

Select **Empty Activity** and click on **Next**.

Customizing your activity

In the last step of the **New Project** wizard, you can customize a little bit of your activity. This customization is going to determine the names of some of your classes and resources files. You can also customize from this wizard the use of fragments or the navigation type.

The following screenshot shows the customization screen for an **Empty Activity**:

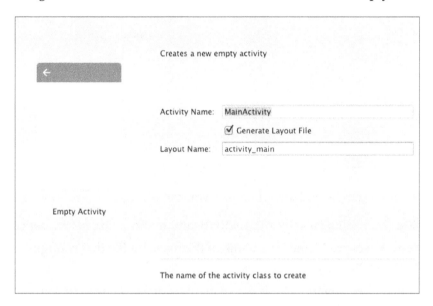

The basic customization for the activity has the following options:

- **Activity Name**: Name of the main activity class.
- **Layout Name**: You can create a layout for your activity if you check the **Generate Layout File** option. This field lets you specify the name of the layout associated with your main activity, which will be created in the resources folder.

Depending on the type of activity selected in the previous steps, you can customize more parameters. The following screenshot shows the customization of **Basic Activity**:

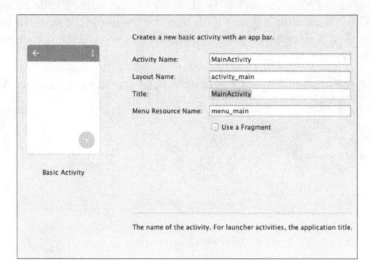

In addition to the activity and layout names, you can configure the following options:

- **Title**: This will be used for the activity and in the action bar by default.
- **Menu Resource Name**: The name of the resource file that configures the menu items.

There are other customizations that are available only to one type of activity, such as **AdMob Ads Activity** and **Tabbed Activity**. The **AdMob Ads Activity** contains one additional option, **Ad Format**, which is the format of the ad. Format can be **Interstitial** or **Banner**. The **Tabbed Activity** includes two additional options: **Fragment Layout Name**, which is the name of the layout associated with the activity's content fragment; and **Navigation Style**, which is the type of navigation. You can choose to navigate by any of the following three alternatives:

- Swiping the views (**Swipe Views**) as shown in the next screenshot:

This type of navigation uses a `ViewPager` component to display the fragments. The `ViewPager` object is configured, in the main activity, with a `SectionsPagerAdapter` object. It provides the fragments that the `ViewPager` needs. In addition to the main layout that contains a `ViewPager`, a fragment layout is also created: `fragment_main.xml`.

- Tabs in the action bar (**Action Bar Tabs**) as shown in the next screenshot:

This type of navigation uses the same components and files as the **Swipe Views** navigation type, plus a `TabLayout` object. The `TabLayout` object needs to receive the `ViewPager` object, which is set in the `onCreate` method of the main activity:

```
TabLayout tabLayout = (TabLayout) findViewById(R.id.tabs);
tabLayout.setupWithViewPager(mViewPager);
```

- Using a spinner in the action bar (**Action Bar Spinner**) as shown in the next screenshot:

This type of navigation uses a `Spinner` component to display the fragments. The `Spinner` object is configured, in the main activity, with `ThemedSpinnerAdapter`. It provides the fragments that the `Spinner` needs. In addition to the main layout that contains `ViewPager`, a fragment layout is also created: `fragment_main.xml`.

To complete this chapter, we select **Empty Activity**. Retain the default values in the customization and click on **Finish**.

An **Empty Activity** will be created in your project. This activity is also configured as the main activity of your application in the `AndroidManifest.xml` file by setting the following intent filter action:

```
<activity
    android:name=".MainActivity"
    android:label="@string/app_name" >
    <intent-filter>
        <action android:name="android.intent.action.MAIN" />
        <category android:name="android.intent.category.LAUNCHER" />
    </intent-filter>
</activity>
```

The `android.intent.action.MAIN` action sets the activity as the main entry point of your application. The `android.intent.category.LAUNCHER` category indicates that the entry point should appear as a top-level application in the launcher. We will examine this `AndroidManifest.xml` file in *Chapter 3, Navigating a Project*.

Summary

We have used the Android Studio wizard to create our first project and have filled the configuration fields. We also went through the different kinds of activities.

In the next chapter, we will go through the different elements of the structure of Android Studio. We will see how to create new classes, add and access libraries, and configure the project.

3
Navigating a Project

Now that you have created your first Android Studio project, you will understand what is going on. Before you start programming, you need to familiarize yourself with the navigation in the project. How is everything structured? Which settings can you change in the project? How can you change these settings and what do they mean?

This chapter is designed to introduce the structure of a project in Android Studio. We will start by understanding the project navigation panel. Then, we will go through the most important folders in our project—build, gen, and libs—and the folders under src/main, and you will learn how to change the project settings.

These are the topics we'll be covering in this chapter:

- The navigation panel
- The project structure
- Changing project properties

The project navigation panel

Initially, no project or file is displayed in the main view of Android Studio, as you can see in the next screenshot. As Android Studio suggests, press *Alt +1*, or *cmd 1* if you are using a Mac, to open the project view. You can also open it by clicking on the **Project** button on the left edge of the screen:

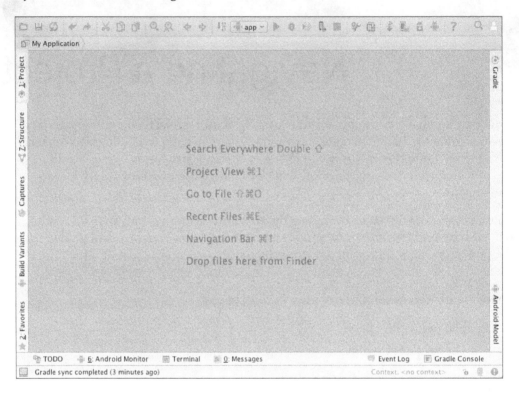

The **Project** view shows the list of the open projects. These projects are displayed in a hierarchical view. We can change the type of view from the upper-left corner of the project explorer. In the upper-right corner of the **Project** view, there are some actions and a drop-down menu to configure the selected type of the **Project** view. These actions are highlighted in the following screenshot:

Open the view selector from the upper-left corner to see the complete list of view types that you can select, which the following screenshot shows:

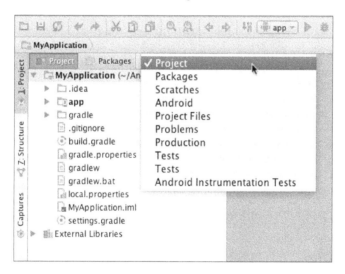

These are the available types of view to navigate through your project:

- **Project**: This view shows the directory structure of the project.
- **Packages**: It shows only the package structure.
- **Scratches**: It shows only the scratches files that you created in your project. Scratch files are runnable and debuggable files that are used for code prototyping. You can create a new scratch file using the menu option by navigating to **Tools | New Scratch File**.

- **Android**: It shows only the folders where you, as a developer, will include or edit your application files. This view is very convenient to easily access all the files that you really need. These folders are related only to the Android application listed in a simplified structure: the `java` classes folder, the `res` resources folder, the `manifest` file, and the Gradle scripts. Since the purpose of this view type is presenting a simplified structure, it doesn't match the real folder structure.

- **Scopes (Project Files, Problems, Production, Tests, and Android Instrumentation Tests)**: Scopes are subsets of your project files, packages, and folders. If you select one of the predefined scopes, you can create your own customized scopes from the configuration menu in the upper-right corner of the **Project** view. Open the configuration menu and select the **Edit Scopes** option. By default, you will see the next predefined scopes:

  - **Project Files**: This scope shows all the files in your project
  - **Problems**: This scope shows all the files with errors in your project
  - **Production**: This scope shows all the files in your project that are not test files
  - **Tests**: This scope shows all the test files
  - **Android Instrumentation Tests**: This scope shows all the instrumented test files

Right-click on the project name to open the context menu or click on any element of the project. As you can see in the following screenshot, from this menu, we can:

- Create and add new elements to the project
- Cut, copy, paste, or rename files in the project
- Find elements in the project
- Analyze and reformat the code
- Build the project
- Compare files
- Open files in Explorer

The project structure

We can examine the project structure in the project navigation pane using the **Project** view type. The project structure includes a folder with the name of our application. This folder contains the application structure and files. The most important elements of the application structure are in the app directory. These include the following:

- build/: This is a folder that contains the resources compiled after building the application and the classes generated by the Android tools, such as the R.java file that contains the references to the application resources.

- libs/: This is a folder that contains the libraries referenced from our code.

- src/androidTest/: This is a folder that contains the test classes of the Java classes that need to be tested.

- `src/main/`: This is a folder that contains the sources of our application. All the files you will usually work with are in this folder. The `main` folder is subdivided as follows:

  - `java/`: This is a folder that contains the Java classes organized as packages. Every class we create will be in our project package namespace (`com.example.myapplication`). When we created our first project, we also created its main activity, so the activity class should be in this package. The next screenshot shows this main activity class inside the project structure:

  - `res/`: This is a folder that contains project resources such as the XML files that specify layouts and menus, or the images files.

  - `AndroidManifest.xml`: This is an essential file in an Android project, which is generated automatically when we create the project. This file declares the basic information needed by the Android system to run the application: package name, version, activities, permissions, intents, or required hardware.

- `build.gradle`: This file is the script used to build our application. We will discuss how to configure options in this file in the *Gradle* subsection of this chapter.

The resources folder

The resources are all non-code assets associated with our application. Elements such as images or strings are externalized from the code as resources, making it easy to update them without changing the code. Some examples of resources include colors, images, graphics, layouts, strings, and styles. The resources are distributed to the following folders:

- `anim/`: This is a folder that contains animation objects as XML files.
- `color/`: This is a folder that contains the color state lists used in our application. The color state lists define colors and color changes based on the component states.
- `drawable/`: This is a folder that contains the images and the XML files describing the drawable objects used in our application.
- `mipmap/`: This is a folder that contains the launcher icons of your app. There are different drawable folders categorized into the different screen densities. When we created our first project, a default application icon was created as well. This icon, named `ic_launcher.png`, is already in these folders.
- `layout/`: This is a folder that contains the XML definitions of the views and their elements.
- `menu/`: This is a folder that contains the XML definitions of the menus for the application.
- `values/`: This is a folder that contains the XML files that define sets of name-value pairs. These values can be colors, strings, or styles. There are different values folders that are categorized into different screen options to adapt the interface to them; for example, to enlarge the components or the fonts when the application is running on a tablet.

Our basic project contains some basic resources. Therefore, all the folders discussed here are not necessarily included by default.

The manifest file

The `AndroidManifest.xml` file is a mandatory file that contains crucial information that the Android system needs about your app. The two essential XML tags that the manifest file must contain are the following:

- `<manifest>`: The root element of the XML file. The `package` attribute defines the Java package name of your app, which is the unique identifier of your app. Other attributes of this element allow you to set the version code (`android:versionCode`) or the version name (`android:versionName`).

- `<application>`: This element in `<manifest>` contains the rest of the elements of your app, such as activities (`<activity>`), services (`<service>`), or content providers (`<provider>`) elements. You can specify several attributes for this element that allow you, for example, to set the app as debuggable (`android:debuggable`), set a user-readable label for the app (`android:label`) or set whether your app allows backup (`android:allowBackup`).

The manifest file also declares the permissions and features that your app needs. For example, if your app needs Internet access, the manifest has to add it into the manifest file:

```
<uses-permission android:name="android.permission.INTERNET" />
```

You can also present information about the SDK to the Android system using the manifest file. Use the `<uses-sdk>` element and its attributes to indicate the minimum SDK version that your app supports and your target SDK.

Gradle

Applications in Android Studio are built using **Gradle**. It is a build automation tool that is independent of Android Studio, but totally integrated with it. Gradle uses an extensible and declarative **domain-specific language** (DSL) that is based on Groovy, which is an object-oriented programming language for the Java platform. A Gradle build file consists of one or more projects, and each project contains one or more tasks. A task represents a piece of work to be built. You can learn more about Gradle at http://www.gradle.org/.

The configuration for the build process is declared in the Gradle build files included in the Android projects. As explained previously, in the project structure, the build configuration file of the Android application is defined in the /app/build.gradle file. Some of the main options we can configure in this file are as follows:

- **Variants**: We can configure different versions of our application using the same project, for example, to create demo and paid versions. The variants depend on the build type (the `buildTypes` tag) and product flavor configurations (the `productFlavors` tag). For example, two build types are `debug` and `release`, and two product flavors are demo and paid versions. In your app's Gradle build file, you will find the `buildType` for release:

```
buildTypes {
    release {

        ...
    }
}
```

- **Dependencies**: We can indicate the local or remote dependencies of our project on other modules or libraries. These dependencies are declared under the `dependencies` tag. In your app's Gradle build file, you will find a dependency to the JAR files contained in the `lib` folder of your project, and to JUnit, the testing framework:

```
dependencies {
    compile fileTree(dir: 'libs', include: ['*.jar'])
    testCompile 'junit:junit:4.12'
}
```

- **Manifest entries**: We can override some entries of the Android manifest file in the build file, providing a dynamic configuration of the `manifest` file. For example, we can override the values of the package name, the minimum SDK, or the target SDK. These configurations are defined under the `android/defaultConfig` tags:

```
defaultConfig {
    applicationId "com.example.myapplication"
    minSdkVersion 16
    targetSdkVersion 23
    versionCode 1
    versionName "1.0"
}
```

- **Signing**: We can activate the application signing for the release version. The build system uses a default certificate to sign the debug version of the application. We can configure our key and certificate to sign the release version as well. These configurations are defined under the `android/signingConfigs` tags. You will learn how to sign your app in *Chapter 9, Preparing for Release*.

Project settings

You can navigate to the two dialogs that contain project settings using **File | Settings** and **File | Project Structure**. Both are also available in the toolbar:

Select your project from the project view and navigate to the **Settings** menu in **File**. The left-hand-side panel of the **Settings** dialog displays the options structured in the following sections:

- **Appearance & Behavior**: You can change the appearance and behavior of Android Studio such as font size, theme, updates, passwords, or scopes management.

- **Keymap**: This manages the keyboard shortcuts.

- **Editor**: This customizes the code editor by selecting colors, using templates or changing the encoding. The default encoding is UTF-8. You will learn more about the **Editor** settings in *Chapter 4, Using the Code Editor*.

- **Plugins**: This manages the plugins. You can install and remove plugins, enable or disable them, or you can check their version.

- **Version Control**: In this section, you can find settings related to version control; for example, you can configure the background execution or add files to ignore. Version control will be explained in more detail in *Chapter 6, Tools*.

- **Build**, **Execution**, **Deployment**: In this section, you can configure the build tools such as Gradle, the compiler, and the debugger.

- **Languages & Frameworks**: These are settings related to the frameworks used in your project.

- **Tools**: This section includes the settings related to other tools. You can manage the web browsers, the terminal, or add server certificates.

Some of these settings are general settings, but some others are only for the current project. You can differentiate the current project settings by the icon that appears next to them, or from the label in the settings header, **For current project**, as the next screenshot shows:

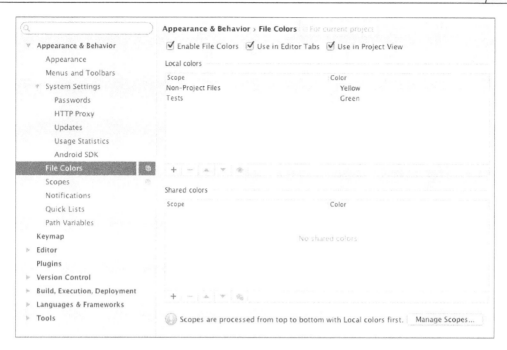

In addition to these **Settings**, there are further settings in the **Project Structure** dialog. Navigate to **File | Project Structure** menu. The settings include the following:

- **SDK Location**: You can change the project SDK. In *Chapter 1, Installing and Configuring Android Studio*, we selected an SDK as the default. In this screen, we can change this SDK, just for the current project.

- **Project**: You can change the Gradle version or the plugin and library repository.

- **Developer Services**: You can configure several developer services in your app. The available services are the following: **Ads** (AdMob), **Analytics** (Google Analytics), **Authentication** (Google Sign-In), **Cloud** (Firebase), and **Notifications** (Google Cloud Messaging).

- **Modules**: According to IntelliJ IDEA (`http://www.jetbrains.com/idea/webhelp/module.html`), the following is the definition of a module:

  > "A module is a discrete unit of functionality which you can compile, run, test, and debug independently."

  This **Modules** menu shows a list of the existing modules with their facets. The default module we have in our project is the app module. The settings tabs correspond to the following Gradle build file configurations: **Properties**, **Signing**, **Flavors**, **Build Types**, and **Dependencies**.

You can add new modules to your project by clicking on the add button in the upper-left corner of the **Project Structure** dialog. This action will open a module selector wizard as shown in the following screenshot:

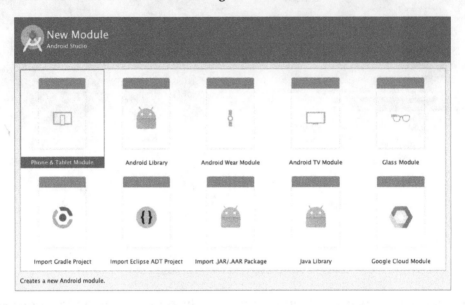

You can select one of the following module types: **Phone & Tablet Module**, **Android Library**, **Android Wear Module**, **Android TV Module**, **Glass Module**, **Import Gradle Project**, **Import Eclipse ADT Project**, **Import .JAR/.AAR Package**, **Java Library**, or **Google Cloud Module**.

Summary

We saw how projects are presented in Android Studio and which folders they contain by default when created. We explored the reasons for having those folders and examined the `AndroidManifest.xml` file and its purpose. We also went through the project settings in the **Preferences** and **Project Structure** dialogs. By now, you should know how to manipulate and navigate through a project in Android Studio.

In the next chapter, we will discuss how to use the text editor. Proper knowledge of the text editor is important in order to improve our programming efficiency. You will learn about the editor settings and how to autocomplete code, use pregenerated blocks of code, and navigate through the code. You will also learn about some useful shortcuts.

Using the Code Editor

4

Now that you have created your first project and learned how to navigate through the different folders, subfolders, and files, it's time to start programming. Have you ever wanted to be able to program more efficiently? How can you speed up your development process? Do you want to learn useful shortcuts too? For example, how can you comment more than one line at once, find and replace strings, or move faster through different parameters in a method call?

In this chapter, you will learn how to use and customize the code editor in order to feel more comfortable when programming. It is worth knowing the basic features of the code editor in order to increase your productivity. You will learn about code completion and code generation. Finally, you will learn some useful shortcuts and hotkeys to speed up the development process.

The following are the topics we'll be covering in this chapter:

* Customizing the code editor
* Code completion
* Code generation
* Finding related content
* Useful shortcuts

Customizing editor settings

To open the editor settings, navigate to **File** | **Settings**. In the **IDE Settings** section of the left panel, select **Editor**. The **Editor** settings are distributed among several categories: **General, Colors & Fonts, Code Style, Inspections, File and Code Templates, File Encodings, Live Templates, File Types, Copyright, Emmet, Images, Intentions, Language Injections, Spelling**, and **TODO**.

We are explaining some of the most interesting ones in this section and in the next sections of this chapter.

General

Select **General** settings under the **Editor** settings. This displays the settings in the right-hand side panel. Some of the most interesting options are the following:

- **Mouse | Change font size (Zoom) with Ctrl + Mouse Wheel**: Checking this option allows us to change the font size of the editor using the mouse wheel, as we do in other programs such as web browsers.

- **Other | Show quick documentation on mouse move**: Checking this option enables the display of a quick document about the code in a small dialog when we move the mouse over a piece of code and wait for 500 milliseconds. You can change the default delay value of 500 milliseconds. When we move the mouse again, the dialog automatically disappears, but if we move the mouse into the dialog, then we can examine the document in detail. This is very useful in order to read what a method does and to identify its parameters without navigating to it. The following screenshot displays this functionality:

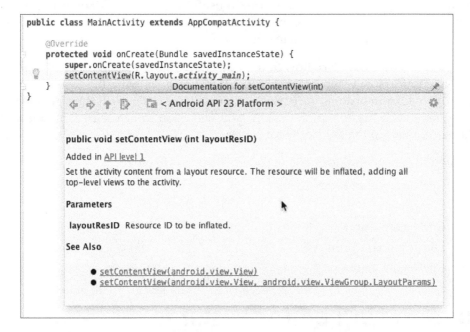

The **General** settings are also distributed among several subcategories:

- **Auto Import**: This category configures how the editor behaves when we paste code that uses classes not imported into the current class. By default, when we do this, a popup appears, and it tells us to add the `import` command. If we check the **Add unambiguous imports on the fly** option, the `import` command is added automatically, without our interaction.

```
 1    package com.example.myapplication;
 2
 3   import android.os.Bundle;
 4    import android.app.Activity;
 5   import android.view.Menu;
 6
 7    public class MainActivity extends Activity {
 8
 9        @Override
10        protected void onCreate(Bundle savedInstanceState) {
11    ? android.util.Log? Alt+Enter  ete(savedInstanceState);
12            setContentView(R.layout.activity_main);
13            Log.i("MainActivity", "Test");|
14        }
```

- **Appearance**: This category configures the appearance of the editor. We recommend checking the next two options:
    - **Show line numbers**: This shows the line numbers on the left edge of the editor. It can be very useful when we are debugging or examining the log.
    - **Show method separators**: This visually separates the methods of a class.

- **Code Completion**: This category configures the code completion options. We will examine code completion in detail in the next section.

- **Code Folding**: This category collapses or expands code blocks allowing us to hide code blocks that we are not editing, simplifying the code view. We can collapse or expand the blocks using the icons from the editor, as shown in the following screenshot, or using the **Folding** menu from **Code**:

```
 1    package com.example.myapplication;
 2
 3   import ...
 6
 7    public class MainActivity extends Activity {
 8
 9        @Override
10        protected void onCreate(Bundle savedInstanceState) {
11            super.onCreate(savedInstanceState);
12            setContentView(R.layout.activity_main);
13        }
14
```

- **Console**: This configures the console. You can modify the commands history size or the lines that are folded.

- **Editor Tabs**: This configures the editor tabs. We advise you to select the **Mark modified tabs with asterisk** option to easily detect modified and unsaved files.

- **Postfix Completion**: This configures a type of code completion called postfix completion. We will examine code completion in detail in the next section.

- **Smart Keys**: This category configures actions to be done automatically while typing, such as adding closing brackets, quotes, or tags, and indenting the line when we press the *Enter* key.

Colors & Fonts

This category changes the fonts and colors. There are a lot of options and elements to configure (keywords, numbers, warnings, errors, comments, strings, and so on). You can save the configurations as schemes from the main screen configuration of the **Color & Fonts** settings.

Code Style

The **Code Style** settings affect only the current project. You can save the style configuration as schemes from the main panel of this settings category. There are several file types that you can configure separately: **C/C++**, **Groovy**, **HTML**, **Java**, **JSON**, **Properties**, **XML**, and other file types.

The following style features are some of the ones that you can configure:

- **Tabs and Indents**: Configure if you want to use tab characters or white spaces (we suggest not using tab characters) and some of their properties, such as size or indentation.

- **Spaces**: Configure the insertion of white spaces before parentheses, around operators, before left braces, before keywords, and so on.

- **Wrapping and Braces**: Configure line breaks, braces placement (for example, **End of line** or **Next line**), argument placement, control statements, and so on.

- **Blank Lines**: Configure the insertion of blank lines, for example, before or after imports, around method bodies, or around fields.

An appropriate code styling makes your code easier to understand. Using a common code styling is very important if the code is written by several developers or if your code is shared with other developers.

File and Code Templates

This category allows you to edit and create templates for files, file headers, or code. The **File and Code Templates** settings affect only the current project. You can save the style configuration as schemes from the main panel of this settings category.

You can change the file header template for your project using some predefined variables that are explained in the detail panel (`${PACKAGE_NAME}`, `${USER}`, `${DATE}`, `${TIME}`, `${PROJECT_NAME}`, and so on).

Click on the **Includes** tab of the **File and Code Templates** settings and select the **File Header** template. Every time you create a new file, the following header is added:

```
/**
 * Created by ${USER} on ${DATE}.
 */
```

You can modify it by adding the file package:

```
/**
 * ${PACKAGE_NAME}
 * Created by ${USER} on ${DATE}.
 */
```

You can also create and modify the templates that are applied when you create a new activity, fragment, service, resource file, and so on. For example, this is the template for an activity:

```
package ${PACKAGE_NAME};

import android.app.Activity;
import android.os.Bundle;

#parse("File Header.java")
public class ${NAME} extends Activity {
    @Override
    public void onCreate(Bundle savedInstanceState) {
        super.onCreate(savedInstanceState);
    }
}
```

You can learn more in the IntelliJ IDEA documentation at `https://www.jetbrains.com/help/idea/2016.1/file-and-code-templates.html`.

Code Completion

Code Completion helps us write code quickly by automatically completing the code using dynamic suggestion lists that are generated based on what we just typed.

The basic code completion is the list of suggestions that appears while we are typing, as shown in the following screenshot. If the list is not displayed, press *Ctrl* and the *Spacebar* to open it:

```
 9        @Override
10        protected void onCreate(Bundle savedInstanceState) {
11            super.onCreate(savedInstanceState);
12            setContentView(R.layout.activity_main);
13
14            L
15        ⌂   LAYOUT_INFLATER_SERVICE                          String
16            LOCATION_SERVICE                                 String
17            LinkageError  (java.lang)
18            Long  (java.lang)
19            databaseList ()                                  String[]
20            fileList ()                                      String[]
21            getClassLoader ()                             ClassLoader
22            getLayoutInflater ()                        LayoutInflater
23            getLoaderManager ()                          LoaderManager
24            getLocalClassName ()                             String
25        }
26        Press Ctrl+Punto to choose the selected (or first) suggestion and insert a dot afterwards >>
```

Keep typing, select a command from the list, and press *Enter* or double-click to add it to your code. If the code you are writing is an expression and you want to insert the expression in its negated form, then select the expression from the suggestion list, and instead of pressing *Enter* or double-clicking it, press the exclamation mark key (*!*). The expression will be added with negation.

Another utility of code completion is the **completion of statements**. Type a statement, press *Ctrl* + *Shift* + *Enter* (*Cmd* + *Shift* + *Enter* on OS X), and notice how the closing punctuation is automatically added. If you press these keys after typing the `if` keyword, the parentheses and brackets are added to complete the conditional statement. This shortcut can also be used to complete method declarations. Start typing a method, and after typing the opening parenthesis or the method parameters, press *Ctrl* + *Shift* + *Enter* (*Cmd* + *Shift* + *Enter* on OS X). The closing parenthesis and the brackets are added to complete the method specification.

Smart Type Completion

Another type of code completion is the **smart type** code completion. If you are typing a command to call a method with a String parameter, then only the String objects will be suggested. This smart completion occurs in the right-hand side of an assignment statement, parameters of a method call, return statements, or variable initializers. To open the smart suggestions list, press *Ctrl + Shift* along with the Spacebar.

To show the difference between these two types of suggestion lists, create two objects of different classes, String and int, in your code. Then call a method with a String parameter, for example, the i method of the Log class. When typing the String parameter, note the difference between opening the basic suggestion list (*Ctrl + Spacebar*), which the next screenshot shows, and open the smart type suggestion list (*Ctrl + Shift + Spacebar*), which the second screenshot shows:

In the first list, which is shown in the previous screenshot, both objects are suggested, although the int object does not match the parameter class. In the second one, which is shown in the following screenshot, only String objects are suggested:

Postfix Completion

The **Postfix Completion** is a type of code completion that transforms an already typed expression. The transformation depends on the postfix you write, the context and the type of expression. Postfix expressions are suggested in the basic code completion suggestion list. One example postfix template is `notnull`, which is the one suggested in the following screenshot:

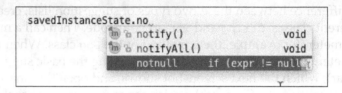

When you apply the `notnull` template to an expression `expr`, the expression is transformed to `if (expr != null)`. The expression from the previous screenshot becomes the next code when the `notnull` transformation is done:

```
if (savedInstanceState != null) {


}
```

If you want to see only the available postfix templates in the suggestion list, press *Ctrl + J* (*Cmd + J* for OS X). A dialog like the one in the next screenshot lists all the available postfix templates that can be applied to the current expression:

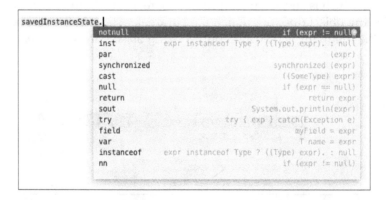

You can manage different postfix templates from the **Editor** settings, in **General | Postfix Completion**. A complete list of all the available templates is displayed along with their description on the right-hand side panel.

The next screenshot shows the description and transformation of the `for` postfix template:

```
Description
  Iterates over enumerable collection.
Before
1 public class Foo {
2     void m() {
3         int[] values = {1, 2, 3};
4         values.for
5     }
6 }
After
1 public class Foo {
2     void m() {
3         int[] values = {1, 2, 3};
4         for (int value : values) {
5
6         }
7     }
8 }
```

Code generation

To generate blocks of code in a class, navigate to **Code** | **Generate** or press the *Alt + Insert* shortcut (*Cmd + N* on OS X). A dialog like the following is displayed:

```
            Generate
  Constructor
  toString()
  Override Methods...      ^O
  Delegate Methods...
  Super Method Call
  Copyright
  App Indexing API Code
```

From the **Generate** menu, you can generate constructors, getters and setters methods, super method calls, or `equals` and `toString` methods. We can also override or delegate methods.

Another way of generating code is surrounding some of our code with statements (if, if/else, while, for, try/catch, and so on). Select a code line and navigate to **Code | Surround With** or press *Ctrl + Alt + T* (*Cmd + Alt + T* on OS X). The menu for the **Surround With** option is shown in the following screenshot:

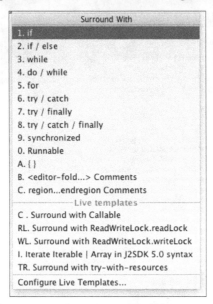

The third option, which is also shown in the previous screenshot, is inserting a **Live Template**. You can surround your code with a **Live Template** using the **Surround With** option or you can navigate to **Code | Surround with Live Templates** or press *Ctrl + Alt + J* (*Cmd + Alt + J* on OS X).

Navigate to **Code | Insert Live Templates** or press *Ctrl + J* (*Cmd + J* on OS X) to open a dialog of the available live templates. These templates can insert code to iterate collections, arrays, lists, and so on; code to print formatted strings; code to throw exceptions; or code to add static and final variables. The left edge of the dialog shows the prefix for each template. If you type the prefix in the editor and press the *Tab* key, the code template is added automatically.

Type inn at the end of the onCreate method of our main activity and press *Tab*. A conditional block will appear. In this new block, type soutv and press *Tab* again. The result is as follows:

```
protected void onCreate(Bundle savedInstanceState) {
    super.onCreate(savedInstanceState);
    setContentView(R.layout.activity_main);
```

```
    if (savedInstanceState != null) {
        System.out.println("savedInstanceState = " +
    savedInstanceState);
    }
}
```

Navigating code

The most direct way of navigating to declarations or type declarations is pressing *Ctrl* (*Cmd* on OS X) and clicking on the method name when it is displayed as a link. This option is also accessible from the **Navigate** | **Declaration** menu or pressing *Ctrl* + *B* (*Cmd* + *B* on OS X).

We can navigate through the hierarchy of methods from the left edge of the editor. Next to the method declarations that belong to a hierarchy of methods, there is an icon that indicates whether a method is implementing an interface method, implementing an abstract class method, overriding a superclass method, or getting implemented or overridden by other descendants. Click on these icons to navigate to the methods in the hierarchy. This option is also available via **Navigate** | **Super Method** or **Navigate** | **Implementation(s)**. You can test it in the main activity of our first project (`MainActivity.java`), as shown in the following screenshot:

On the left edge of the editor, you can find another type of navigation icon. Open your main activity class to see the **Go to Related Files** icon, as the next screenshot shows:

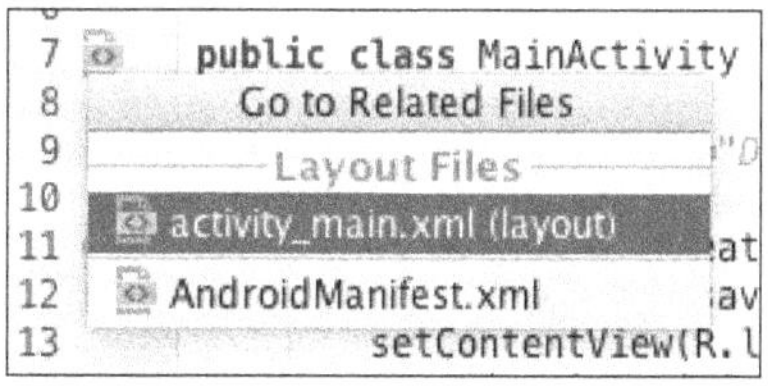

From the **Go to Related Files** menu, you can navigate to files and classes related to the current one. In this example, the related files are the layout associated to your activity and the app manifest file.

Another useful utility related to code navigation is the use of **custom regions**. A custom region is a piece of code that you want to group and name. For example, if there is a class with many methods, we can create some custom regions to distribute the methods among them. A region has a name or description, and it can be collapsed or expanded using code folding.

To create a custom region, we can use the code generation. Select the fragment of code, navigate to **Code | Surround With**, and select one of these two options:

- **<editor-fold...> Comments**
- **region...endregion Comments**

Both of these options create a region but use different styles.

When we are using custom regions, we can navigate to them using the **Custom Folding** menu in **Navigate**. The rest of the navigation options are accessible from the **Navigate** menu. Some of these options are as follows:

- **Class/File/Symbol**: This finds a class, file, or symbol by its name.
- **Line**: This option goes to a line of code by its number.
- **Last Edit Location**: This navigates to the most recent change point.
- **Test**: This navigates to the test of the current class.
- **File Structure**: This opens a dialog that shows the file structure. Open the file structure of our main activity and observe how the structure is presented, displaying the list of methods and the icons that indicate the type or visibility of the element, as shown in the following screenshot:

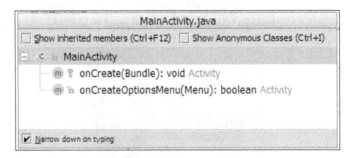

- **Type Hierarchy**: This opens a dialog that shows the type hierarchy of the selected object.

- **Method Hierarchy**: This opens a dialog that shows the method hierarchy of the selected method.

- **Call Hierarchy**: This opens a dialog that shows the call hierarchy of the selected method.

- **Next Highlighted Error**: This navigates to the next error.

- **Previous Highlighted Error**: This navigates to the previous error.

- **Next Method**: This navigates to the next method.

- **Previous Method**: This navigates to the previous method.

Useful shortcuts

You can find all the available shortcuts and change them through the **Keymap** option in the **Settings**. If you double-click on the actions, the **Edit Shortcuts** menu is displayed. From this menu, you can remove the shortcut or add a new one, which can be a keyboard shortcut, a mouse shortcut, or an abbreviation.

Some useful shortcuts for Windows and OS X are included in the following list:

- *Ctrl + W* (*Alt* + Up arrow on OS X): This selects expressions based on grammar. Press these keys repeatedly to expand the selection. The opposite command is *Ctrl + Shift + W* (*Alt* + Up arrow on OS X).

- *Ctrl + /* (*Cmd + /* on OS X): This comments each line of the selected code. To block comments, use *Ctrl + Shift + /* (*Alt + Cmd + /* on OS X).

- *Ctrl + Alt + I*: This indents the selected code. This is useful when cleaning up a block of code or method after you finish writing.

- *Ctrl + Alt + O*: This optimizes the imports, removes the unused imports, and reorders the rest of them.

- *Shift + Ctrl +* Arrows (*Alt + Shift +* Arrows on OS X): This moves the selected code a line above or below.

- *Alt +* Arrows (*Ctrl +* Arrows on OS X): This switches between the opened tabs of the editor.

- *Ctrl + F* (*Cmd + F* on OS X): This finds a string in the active tab of the editor.

- *Ctrl + R* (*Cmd + R* on OS X): This replaces a string in the active tab of the editor.

- *Ctrl + A* (*Cmd + A* on OS X): This selects all of the code of the opened file.

- *Ctrl + D* (*Cmd + D* on OS X): This copies the selected code and pastes it at the end of the selection. If no code is selected, then the entire line is copied and pasted in a new line.

- *Ctrl + Y* (*Cmd + Delete* on OS X): This removes the entire line without leaving a blank line.

- *Ctrl + Shift + U* (*Cmd + Shift + U* on OS X): This toggles the case.

- *Ctrl + O* (*Cmd + O* on OS X): This opens a search box to navigate through project classes.

- *Ctrl + Shift + O* (*Cmd + Shift + O* on OS X): This opens a search box to navigate through project files.

- *Ctrl + Shift + A* (*Cmd + Shift + A* on OS X): This opens a search box to navigate through available actions on the IDE.

- *Tab*: This moves to the next parameter.

Summary

By the end of this chapter, you should have learned some useful tricks and tips to make the most of the code editor. You know now how to use code completion, code generation, and some useful shortcuts for speeding up different actions. We also customized our code editor and are now ready to start programming.

In the next chapter, we will start creating our first user interface using layouts. You will learn how to create a layout using the graphical wizard, as well as by editing the XML layout file using the text-based view. We will create our first application, a classic *Hello World* example, using the text view component. You will also learn how to prepare our application for multiple screen sizes and adapt them for different device orientations. Finally, you will learn about UI themes and how to handle events.

Downloading the example code

Code Detailed steps to download the code bundle are mentioned in the Preface of this book. The code bundle for the book is also hosted on GitHub at `https://github.com/PacktPublishing/Android-Studio-2-Essentials-Second-Edition/tree/master`. We also have other code bundles from our rich catalog of books and videos available at `https://github.com/PacktPublishing/`. Check them out!

5
Creating User Interfaces

Now that we created our first project and have become familiar with the code editor and its functionalities, we will begin our application by creating our user interface. Is there more than one way to create a user interface using Android Studio? How can you add components to your user interface? Have you ever wondered how to make your applications support different screen sizes and resolutions?

This chapter focuses on the creation of the user interfaces using layouts. Layouts can be created using a graphical view or a text-based view. You will learn how to use both of them to create your layout. We will also code a `Hello World` application using simple components. Since there are over 18,000 Android device types, you will learn about fragmentation on different screen types and we will discuss how to prepare our application for this issue. We will end this chapter with basic notions of handling events in our application.

These are the topics we'll be covering in this chapter:

- Existing layout editors
- Creating a new layout
- Adding components
- Supporting different screens
- Changing the UI theme
- Handling events

The graphical editor

Open the main layout located at `/src/main/res/layout/activity_main.xml` in our project. The graphical editor will be opened by default. The center panel of the graphical editor is the **Preview**, where you can examine what your layout looks like. From the **Preview** you can see that initially this main layout contains just a text view with a **Hello World!** message. To switch between the graphical and text editors, click on the **Design** and **Text** tabs at the bottom of the screen, as shown in the screenshot:

The **Toolbar** options contains some options that can be used to change the layout style and preview. The **Toolbar** options, which are shown in the following screenshot, are explained throughout the chapter:

The **Component Tree** panel displays the components placed in the layout as a hierarchy. There are two components in our layout: a **RelativeLayout** as the root element, and a **TextView** which is the one displaying the **Hello World!** message. When you select one element on the **Component Tree** panel, the element is highlighted in **Preview**, and its properties are listed in the **Properties** inspector panel. It shows the properties of the selected component from the layout and allows us to change them. **Palette** lists the existing **user interface** (**UI**) components to place in our layout. It organizes the components in different categories. Let's look at the options available in **Components Palette**:

- **Layouts**: A layout is a container object used to distribute the components on the screen. The root element of UI is a layout object, but layouts can also contain more layouts, creating a hierarchy of components structured in layouts. The recommendation is to keep this layout hierarchy as simple as possible. Our main layout has **RelativeLayout** as a root element.

- **Widgets**: This category contains options for text views, buttons, checkboxes, switches, image views, progress bars, seek bars, rating bars, spinners, and web views. They are the most commonly used components, and they are used in most layouts. Our main layout contains **TextView** inside the root relative layout.

- **Text Fields**: These are editable fields that contain different categories of input under which users can type text. The difference between the various options is the type of text users can type.

- **Containers**: This category groups components that share a common behavior. Radio groups, list views, grid views, scroll views, and tab hosts are some of them.

- **Date & Time**: This category holds components related to date and time in the form of calendars or clocks.

- **Expert**: The components in this category are not as common as the components in the **Widgets** category, but it is worth taking a look at them.

- **Custom**: This category holds components that allow us to include our custom components, which are usually other layouts from our project.

The text-based editor

Change the graphical editor to the text editor by clicking on the **Text** tab:

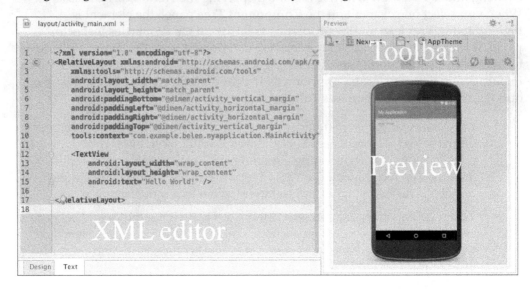

The **Toolbar** panel is the same as that on the graphical editor. The **Preview** window displays the layout, but it cannot be changed. To do that, you should use the **Design** tab instead. The components are added to the layout using their XML declarations. The properties are also configured using XML declarations. Like the graphical editor, the text editor contains two XML elements: a relative layout as the root element and the text view element inside the root layout.

The XML tag names define the type of component that we are declaring. For the relative layout, we use the `RelativeLayout` tag, and for the text view, we use the `TextView` tag. We can add properties to the elements by including attributes in the XML tags. For example, the text view in our main layout has three properties:

- `android:layout_width`, with the `wrap_content` value: This property sets the element width inside its parent element. The `wrap_content` value means that the element's width will be determined by the width of its content. The other default value that you can set for this property is `match_parent`, which means that the element will have the same width as its parent element.

- `android:layout_height`, the `wrap_content` value: This property sets the element height inside its parent element. The values behave the same way as the width.

- `android:text`, with the `Hello World!` value: This property sets the text to be displayed in the text view.

Creating a new layout

When we created our main activity, the associated layout was also created. This is a way of creating a layout when creating an activity.

To add an independent layout without creating a new activity, right-click on the `layout` folder (`res/layout/`) and navigate to **New | Layout resource file**. You can also create a layout file using the same right-click menu by navigating to the **New | XML | Layout XML file**. You can also navigate to these two options using the top **File** menu. The following dialog from the next screenshot will be displayed to configure the new layout component:

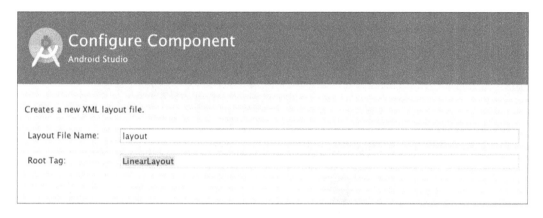

Type the **Layout File Name** and the **Root Tag**. The root element of our main layout was a relative layout, but you can select a different root tag. There are five types of layout:

- **FrameLayout**: This layout displays usually only one child in an arranged area of the screen. If more than one child is added, then the views are displayed in a stack.

- **LinearLayout**: This layout displays its children by aligning them, one after other, in one direction. There are two types of linear layouts: vertical and horizontal, which are identified by the `android:orientation` property of the layout.

- **TableLayout**: This layout displays its children by distributing them in rows and columns. Along with the table layout, you need to use the **TableRow** element to create the distribution in rows and columns.

- **GridLayout**: This layout displays its children in a rectangular grid. Children can fill more than one cell using properties such as `rowSpec` and `columnSpec`.

- **RelativeLayout**: This layout displays its children by the relative positions between them. You have to use the position properties in the children's views to determine their position. At least one child view needs to have a position property relative to the parent view, so that child view, and the ones relative to it, can be positioned inside the parent layout. Some of these properties are `android:layout_below`, `android:layout_toLeftOf`, or `android:layout_alignBottom`.

Once the layout is created, the associated activity can be changed to a different activity using the editor. If the layout has no activity, any existing one can be linked to it from the editor. To accomplish this, search for the **Associate with Activity** option in the toolbar of the layout editor, click on it, and select the **Associate with other Activity** option, as shown in the following screenshot:

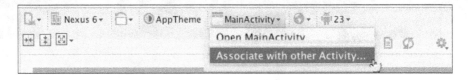

A dialog box that lists all the activities of your project will open, and you can select one of them.

Adding components

Our main layout is a relative layout and contains a text view saying **Hello World!**. Now let's add a new component. The easiest way to do this is using the graphical editor, so open the **Design** tab. Select a component and drag it into the layout preview; for example, navigate to the **Person Name** component in **Text Fields** and place it below the text view.

Since our root layout is a relative layout, as you drag the element in the layout, some line guides are displayed. The properties related to the position are also shown in the top part of the **Preview** as you try to drag and drop the element in the layout. These lines and suggested properties, which are shown in the following screenshot, can help you properly align the element in your screen. They also help you to set the element position relative to the rest of the elements that are already in the layout.

The properties suggested in the **Preview** panel from the previous screenshot align the text field to the left of the parent element (**alignParentLeft**), set the text field position below the **Hello World!** text view (**below=textView**), and add a margin to the text view of 38 dp (**margin=38 dp**).

In the **Component Tree** view, there is now a new editText object. Keep the text field selected to examine its properties loaded in the **Properties** inspector. Let's change some of them and observe the differences in the layout preview and in **Component Tree**:

- **layout:width**: This option will adapt the width of the field to its content. Its current value is wrap_content. Change it to match_parent to adapt it to the parent layout width (the root relative layout).

- **hint**: Type Enter your name as the hint of the field. The hint is a text shown when the field is empty to indicate the information that should be typed. As the field has a default value, Name, the hint is not visible.

- **id**: This has `@+id/editText` as the current ID. The ID will be used from the code to get access to this object and is the ID displayed in the component tree. This ID can also be used by other elements in the layout to determine their relative position to it. Change it to `@+id/editText_name` to distinguish it easily from other text fields. Check whether the component ID has also changed in the **Component Tree** window, as shown in the following screenshot:

- **text**: This deletes the value of this field. The hint should now be visible.

If we switch to the text editor, we can see the XML definition of the text field with the properties we edited:

```
<EditText
    android:layout_width="match_parent"
    android:layout_height="wrap_content"
    android:inputType="textPersonName"
    android:ems="10"
    android:id="@+id/editText_name"
    android:layout_marginTop="38dp"
    android:layout_below="@+id/textView"
    android:layout_alignParentLeft="true"
    android:hint="Enter your name"
/>
```

There is a recommended order for the properties of the XML definitions. Having a specific order helps to understand the code when reading it and makes it easier to modify the elements. Select the `EditText` code definition and execute the **Reformat Code** action in the **Code** menu. The properties order has now changed, placing the `android:id` at the first position:

```
<EditText
    android:id="@+id/editText_name"
    android:layout_width="match_parent"
```

```
        android:layout_height="wrap_content"
        android:layout_alignParentLeft="true"
        android:layout_below="@+id/textView"
        android:layout_marginTop="38dp"
        android:ems="10"
        android:hint="Enter your name"
        android:inputType="textPersonName"
/>
```

You can check the position properties (android:layout_marginTop, android:layout_below, and android:layout_alignParentLeft) that match the properties displayed in the graphical editor while you were dragging the edit text in the layout. Note that the android:layout_below property uses the ID of the text view to identify it.

From the text editor, the existing components and their properties can also be changed. Modify the text view ID (the android:id property) from @+id/textView to @+id/textView_greeting. Having a descriptive ID is important since it will be used by our code. Descriptive variable names allow the code to be self-documenting. You will need to change all the references to the text view ID to the new ID.

Let's add another component using the text editor this time. Press the **Open Tag** key and start typing Button. A list of suggestions will appear to help you with the code completion. Let the list of suggestions appear and select a Button object. Inside the Button tag, add the following properties:

- android:id, with the @+id/button_accept value: This creates the ID property.

- android:layout_width, with the wrap_content value: This lets the width adapt to the button content.

- android:layout_height, with the wrap_content value: This lets the height adapt to the button content.

- android:layout_below, with the @id/editText_name value: This places the button below the name text field. We reference the name text field by its ID (@id/editText_name).

- android:layout_centerHorizontal, with the value true: This centers the button horizontally in the parent layout.

- android:text, with the Accept value: This sets the text of the button. The recommended way to add a text to a component is by adding it to the strings.xml file. The component should be configured with the string identifier, instead of the string directly. For simplicity, we are adding the string directly to the button.

The final XML definition for the button is the following:

```
<Button
  android:id="@+id/button_accept"
  android:layout_width="wrap_content"
  android:layout_height="wrap_content"
  android:layout_below="@+id/editText_name"
  android:layout_centerHorizontal="true"
  android:text="Accept"
/>
```

The button is displayed in **Preview**. The next screenshot shows that if we switch to the graphical editor, the button is displayed in it and also in **Component Tree**:

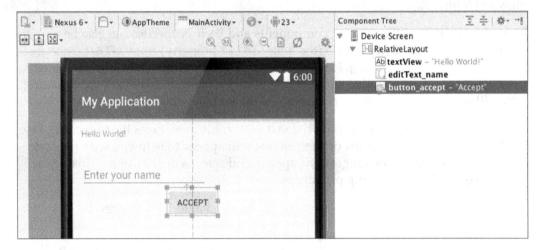

Component's properties

The properties that we added or modified in our main layout can also be modified by code, and not only using the layout editor. For example, if you have a Button object in your code, you can change its text using the setText method:

```
myButton.setText("Accept");
```

Some of the properties available for a View object are the following:

- android:alpha: This XML property sets the alpha value of the view, between 0 and 1, which represents the opacity of the view. You can also use the setAlpha method from code.

- android:background: This XML property sets the background of the view. You can also use the setBackground method from code.

- `android:clickable`: This XML property sets whether the view is clickable or not, receiving the click events or not. You can also use the `setClicklable` method from code.

- `android:elevation`: This XML property sets the elevation value of the view, its z depth value. You can also use the `setElevation` method from code.

- `android:fadeScrollbars`: This XML property sets whether the scroll bars fade out when they are not in use. You can also use the `setScrollbarFadingEnabled` method from code.

- `android:focusable`: This XML property sets whether the view can take the focus or not. You can also use the setFocusable method from code.

- `android:foreground`: This XML property sets the foreground of the view. You can also use the `setForeground` method from code.

- `android:foregroundTint`: This XML property sets the tint color for the foreground of the view. You can also use the `setForegroundTintList` method from code.

- `android:id`: This XML property sets the identifier of the view. You can also use the `setId` method from code.

- `android:minHeight`: This XML property sets the minimum height that the view should have. You can also use the `setMinimumHeight` method from code.

- `android:minWidth`: This XML property sets the minimum width that the view should have. You can also use the `setWidth` method from code.

- `android:padding`: This XML property sets the padding for the four edges of the view. You can also use the `setPadding` method from code. Similar to this property are: `android:paddingBottom`, `android:paddingEnd`, `android:paddingLeft`, `android:paddingRight`, `android:paddingStart`, and `android:paddingTop`.

- `android:scrollIndicators`: This XML property sets whether the scroll indicators are shown for the view. You can also use the `setScrollIndicators` method from code.

- `android:textAlignment`: This XML property sets the alignment of the text in the view. You can also use the `setTextAlignment` method from code.

- `android:visibility`: This XML property sets whether the view is visible or not. You can also use the `setVisibility` method from code.

In addition to the properties of a `View` object, `View` subclasses can provide some more specific properties. For example, the `TextView` objects also have these properties: `android:editable`, `android:fontFamily`, `android:hint`, `android:text`, or `android:textColor`.

Supporting multiple screens

When creating Android applications, we have to take into account the existence of multiple screen sizes and screen resolutions. It is important to check how our layouts are displayed in different screen configurations. To accomplish this, Android Studio provides a functionality to change the virtual device that renders the layout preview when we are in the **Design** mode.

We can find this functionality in the toolbar and click on it to open the list of available device definitions, as shown in the following screenshot:

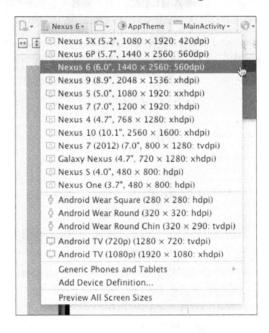

Try some of them. The difference between a tablet device and a device like those from the Nexus line is very notable. We should adapt the views to all the screen configurations our application supports to ensure that they are displayed optimally. Note that there are device definitions for Android Wear (**square**, **round**, and **round chin** designs) and for Android TV.

The device definitions indicate the screen size, resolution, and screen density. Android screen densities include ldpi, mdpi, tvdpi, hdpi, xhdpi, and even xxhdpi. Let's see what their values are:

- **ldpi** : This is **low-density dots per inch**, and its value is about 120 dpi

- **mdpi**: This is **medium-density dots per inch**, and its values is about 160 dpi

- **tvdpi**: This is **medium-density dots per inch**, and its value is about 213 dpi

- **hdpi**: This is **high-density dots per inch**, and its value is about 240 dpi

- **xhdpi**: This is **extra-high-density dots per inch**, and its value is about 320 dpi

- **xxhdpi**: This is **extra-extra-high-density dots per inch**, and its value is about 480 dpi

- **xxxhdpi**: This is **extra-extra-extra-high-density dots per inch**, and its value is about 640 dpi

The last dashboards published by Google show that most devices have high-density screens (42.3 percent), followed by xhdpi (24.8 percent) and xxhdpi (15.0 percent). Therefore, we can cover 82.1 percent of all the devices by testing our application using these three screen densities. If you want to cover a bigger percentage of devices, test your application using mdpi screens (12.9 percent) as well so the coverage will be 95.0 percent of all devices. The official Android dashboards are available at http://developer.android.com/about/dashboards.

Another issue to keep in mind is the **device orientation**. Do we want to support the landscape mode in our application? If the answer is yes, then we have to test our layouts in landscape orientation. On the toolbar, click on the **layout state** option to change the mode either from portrait to landscape or from landscape to portrait.

If our application supports landscape mode and the layout does not get displayed as expected in this orientation, we might want to create a variation of the layout. Click on the first icon of the toolbar, that is, the **Configuration to render this layout with inside the IDE** option, and select the **Create Landscape Variation** option, as shown in the next screenshot:

A new layout will be opened in the editor. This layout has been created in the `resources` folder, under the `layout-land` directory, and it uses the same name as the portrait layout - `/src/main/res/layout-land/activity_main.xml`. The Android system will decide which version of the layout needs to be used depending on the current device orientation. Now, we can edit the new layout variation so that it perfectly conforms to landscape mode.

Similarly, we can create a variation of the layout for extra-large screens. Select the **Create layout-xlarge Variation** option. The new layout will be created in the `layout-xlarge` folder using the same name as the original layout at `/src/main/res/layout-xlarge/activity_main.xml`. Android divides into actual screen sizes of small, normal, large, and extra large:

- **Small**: Screens classified in this category are at least 426 dp x 320 dp.
- **Normal**: Screens classified in this category are at least 470 dp x 320 dp.
- **Large**: Screens classified in this category are at least 640 dp x 480 dp.
- **Extra large**: Screens classified in this category are at least 960 dp x 720 dp.

A **density-independent pixel (dp)** is equivalent to one physical pixel on a 160 dpi screen. The latest dashboards published by Google show that most devices have a normal screen size (85.1 percent), followed by large screen size (8.2 percent). The official Android dashboards are available at `http://developer.android.com/about/dashboards`.

To display multiple device configurations at the same time, click on the **Configuration to render this layout with inside the IDE** option in the toolbar and select the **Preview All Screen Sizes** option, or click on the **Preview Representative Sample** option to open only the most important screen sizes, as shown in the following screenshot. We can also delete any of the samples by right-clicking on them and selecting the **Delete** option from the menu. Another useful action of this menu is the **Save screenshot** option. It allows us to take a screenshot of the layout preview:

If we create different layout variations, we can preview all of them by selecting the **Preview Layout Versions** option. If we want to preview what the layout looks like for different Android versions, we can use the **Preview Android Versions** option.

Now that we have seen how to add different components and optimize our layout for different screens, let's start working with themes.

Changing the UI theme

Layouts and widgets are created using the default UI theme of our project. We can change the appearance of the elements of the UI by creating styles. Styles can be grouped to create a theme, and a theme can be applied to an activity or to the whole application. Some themes are provided by default, such as the **Material Design** or **Holo** style. Styles and themes are created as resources under the /src/res/values folder.

To continue our example, we are going to change the default colors of the theme that we are using in our app. Using the graphical editor, you can see that the selected theme for our layout is shown as **AppTheme** in the toolbar. This theme was created for our project and can be found in the styles file at /src/res/values/styles.xml.

Open the styles file. Android Studio suggests we use the **Theme Editor**. You can click on the message link or you can navigate to **Tools | Android | Theme Editor** to open it. You can see the **Theme Editor** in the next screenshot:

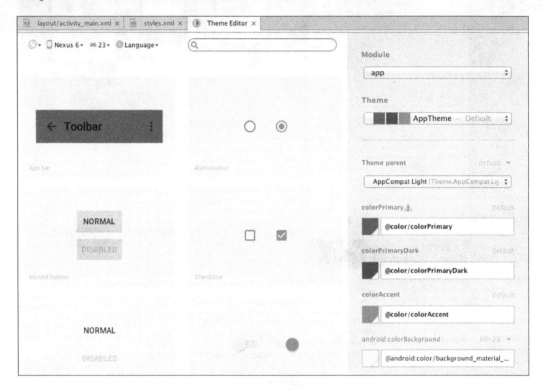

The left panel shows what different UI components look like. For example, you can view the appearance of the app bar, different types of buttons, text views, or the appearance of the status bar. The right panel of the **Theme Editor** contains the settings of the theme. You can change the values from the right panel and see how the components change in the left panel of **Theme Editor**.

In the right-hand configuration panel, you can change the **Theme** to modify, you can change the **Theme parent** of the selected theme, and you can change the theme colors. You will note that **AppTheme** is by default an extension of another theme, Theme.AppCompat.Light.DarkActionBar.

Let's try to change the main color of our app. Follow the next steps:

1. Look for the **colorPrimary** property on the right panel of the **Theme Editor**.

2. Click on the color square of the **colorPrimary** property. The color selector of the following screenshot will be opened:

3. Select a different color and click on the **OK** button. Note that the theme has changed and now the app bar has the new color in **Theme Editor**.

4. Open your main layout file. The preview of the layout has also changed its color. This theme primary color will be applied to all our layouts due to the fact that we configured it in the theme and not just in the layout.

The specification of the colors is saved in the `colors` file at `/src/res/values/` `colors.xml`. This is the current content of the `colors` file:

```
<resources>
    <color name="colorPrimary">#009688</color>
    <color name="colorPrimaryDark">#303F9F</color>
    <color name="colorAccent">#FF4081</color>
</resources>
```

You can also change the colors from this file. Modify the `colorPrimaryDark`, save the file, and note that in the **Theme Editor**, the status bar color has changed to the new color. Switch to your main layout file and observe that the preview of your layout has also changed to show the new color in the status bar.

To change the layout theme completely, click on the theme option from the toolbar in the graphical editor. The theme selector dialog is now opened, displaying a list of the available themes, as shown in the following screenshot:

The themes created in our own project are listed in the **Project Themes** section. The **Manifest Themes** section shows the theme configured in the application manifest file (`/src/main/AndroidManifest.xml`). The **All** section lists all the available themes.

Handling events

The user interface would be useless if the rest of the application could not interact with it. Events in Android are generated when the user interacts with our application. All the UI widgets are children of the `View` class, and they share some events handled by the following listeners:

- `OnClickListener`: This captures the event when the user clicks on the view element. To configure this listener in a view, use the `setOnClickListener` method. The `OnClickListener` interface declares the following method to receive the click event:

  ```
  public abstract void onClick(View v)
  ```

- `OnCreateContextMenu`: This captures the event when the user performs a long click on the view element and we want to open a context menu. To configure this listener in a view, use the `setOnCreateContextMenu` method. The `OnCreateContextMenu` interface declares the following method to receive the long-click event:

  ```
  public abstract void onCreateContextMenu(ContextMenu menu, View v,
  ContextMenu.ContextMenuInfo menuInfo)
  ```

- `OnDragListener`: This captures the event when the user drags and drops the event element. To configure this listener in a view, use the `setOnDragListener` method. The `OnDragListener` interface declares the following method to receive the drag event:

  ```
  public abstract boolean onDrag(View v, DragEvent event)
  ```

- `OnFocusChangedListener`: This captures the event when the user navigates from an element to another in the same view. To configure this listener in a view, use the `setOnFocusChangedListener` method. The `OnFocusChangedListener` interface declares the following method to receive the change of focus event:

  ```
  public abstract void onFocusChange(View v, boolean hasFocus)
  ```

- `OnHoverListener`: This captures the event when the user is moving over an element. To configure this listener in a view, use the `setOnHoverListener` method. The `OnHoverListener` interface declares the following method to receive the hover event:

  ```
  public abstract boolean onHover(View v, MotionEvent event)
  ```

- OnKeyListener: This captures the event when the user presses any key while the view element has the focus. To configure this listener in a view, use the setOnKeyListener method. The OnKeyListener interface declares the following method to receive the key event:

```
public abstract boolean onKey(View v, int keyCode, KeyEvent event)
```

- OnLayoutChangeListener: This captures the event when the layout of a view changes its bounds due to layout processing. To configure this listener in a view, use the setOnLayoutChangeListener method. The OnLayoutChangeListener interface declares the following method to receive the layout change event:

```
public abstract void onLayoutChange(View v,
int left, int top, int right, int bottom,
int oldLeft, int oldTop, int oldRight, int oldBottom)
```

- OnLongClickListener: This captures the event when the user touches the view element and holds it. To configure this listener in a view, use the setOnLongClickListener method. The OnLongClickListener interface declares the following method to receive the long click event:

```
public abstract boolean onLongClick(View v)
```

- OnScrollChangeListener: This captures the event when the scroll position of a view changes. To configure this listener in a view, use the setOnScrollChangeListener method. The OnScrollChangeListener interface declares the following method to receive the scroll change event:

```
public abstract void onScrollChange(View v,
int scrollX, int scrollY,
int oldScrollX, int oldScrollY)
```

- OnTouchListener: This captures the event when the user touches the view element. To configure this listener in a view, use the setOnTouchListener method. The OnTouchListener interface declares the following method to receive the touch event:

```
public abstract boolean onTouch(View v, MotionEvent event)
```

In addition to these standard events and listeners, some UI widgets have some more specific events and listeners. Checkboxes can register a listener to capture when its state changes (OnCheckedChangeListener), and spinners can register a listener to capture when an item is clicked (OnItemClickListener).

The most common event to capture is when the user clicks on the view elements. There is an easy way to handle it—using the view properties. Select the **Accept** button in our layout and look for the onClick property. This property indicates the name of the method that will be executed when the user presses the button. This method has to be created in the activity associated with the current layout, our main activity (MainActivity.java) in this case. Type onAcceptClick as the value of this property.

Open the main activity to create the method definition. When a view is clicked, the event callback method when has to be public with a void return type. It receives the view that has been clicked on as parameter. This method will be executed every time the user clicks on the button:

```
public void onAcceptClick(View v) {
  // Action when the button is pressed
}
```

From the main activity, we can interact with all the components of the interface, so when the user presses the **Accept** button, our code can read the text from the name field and change the greeting to include the name in it.

To get the reference to a view object, use the findViewById method inherited from the Activity class. This method receives the ID of the component and returns the View object corresponding to that ID. The returned view object has to be cast to its specific class in order to use its methods, such as the getText method of the EditText class, to get the name typed by the user:

```
public void onAcceptClick(View v) {
  TextView tvGreeting =
    (TextView) findViewById(R.id.textView_greeting);
  EditText etName = (EditText) findViewById(R.id.editText_name);

  if(0 < etName.getText().length()) {
    tvGreeting.setText("Hello " + et_name.getText());
  }
}
```

In the first two lines of the method, the references to the elements of the layout are retrieved: the text view that contains the greeting and the text field where the user can type a name. The components are found by their IDs, the same ID that we indicated in the properties of the element in the layout file. All the IDs of resources are included in the R class. The R class is autogenerated in the build phase and therefore we must not edit it. If this class is not autogenerated, then probably some file of our resources contain an error.

The next line is a conditional statement used to check whether the user typed a name. If they typed a name, the text will be replaced by a new greeting that contains that name. In the coming chapters, you will learn how to execute our application in an emulator, and we will be able to test this code.

If the event we want to handle is not the user's click, then we have to create and add the listener by code to the onCreate method of the activity. There are two ways to do this:

- Implementing the listener interface in the activity and then adding the unimplemented methods. The methods required by the interface are the methods used to receive the events.

- Creating a private anonymous implementation of the listener in the activity file. The methods that receive the events are implemented in this object.

Finally, the listener implementation has to be assigned to the view element using the setter methods, such as setOnClickListener, setOnCreateContextMenu, setOnDragListener, setOnFocusChange, setOnKeyListener, and so forth. The listener assignment is usually included in the onCreate method of the activity. If the listener is implemented in the same activity, then the parameter indicated to the setter method is the own activity using the this keyword, as shown in the following code:

```
Button bAccept = (Button) findViewById(R.id.button_accept);
bAccept.setOnClickListener(this);
```

The activity should then implement the listener and the onClick method required by the listener interface:

```
public class MainActivity extends Activity
implements View.OnClickListener {
  @Override
  public void onClick(View view) {
    // Action when the button is pressed
  }
```

If we implement it using a private anonymous class, the code would be the following:

```
bAccept.setOnClickListener(new View.OnClickListener() {
    @Override
    public void onClick(View v) {
        // Action when the button is pressed
    }
});
```

Summary

In this chapter, we saw how to create and edit the user interface layouts using both the graphical and the text-based editors. We finished our first small application, and we upgraded it with some basic components. You should now be able to create a simple layout and test it with different styles, screen sizes, and screen resolutions. You also learned about the different available UI themes. Finally, you learned about events and learned how to handle them using listeners.

In the next chapter, you will learn about some useful tools available in the Android Studio. We will use the SDK Manager frequently to install different packages. You will also learn about the AVD Manager for different virtual devices to test your applications on. We will generate Javadoc documentation for our project using the Javadoc utility, and you will learn about the version control systems available in Android Studio.

6
Tools

In the previous chapter, you learned about the useful services that Google provides, which can be used by developers to improve their applications. Now, you will learn about tools available in Android Studio that make your life easier. Have you wondered how to manage the Android platforms? Do you want to have your project clearly documented? Are you working as a group of developers and need a version control manager integrated with Android Studio?

This chapter describes the most important additional tools provided in Android Studio: Android SDK tools, Javadoc, and version control integration. First, you will learn about the SDK Manager available in Android Studio from which you'll be able to examine, update, and install different components for our project. Next, we will review the **Android Virtual Device (AVD)** Manager, where we can edit the virtual devices in which we will be testing our project. You will also learn how to have complete documentation using the Javadoc tool, how to have version control using the systems available in Android Studio, and how to handle your project tasks.

These are the topics we'll be covering in this chapter:

- SDK Manager
- AVD Manager
- Javadoc
- Version control
- Tasks and contexts

Software Development Kit Manager

The SDK Manager is an Android tool accessible from Android Studio to control our Android SDK installation. From this tool, we can examine the Android platforms installed in our system, update them, install new platforms, or install some other components such as Google Play services or Android Support Library.

To open the SDK Manager from Android Studio, navigate to **Tools** | **Android** | **SDK Manager**. You can also click on the shortcut from the toolbar. The SDK Manager is an independent Android tool that has been integrated in Android Studio default settings at **Appearance & Behavior** | **System Settings** | **Android SDK**, as shown in the next screenshot:

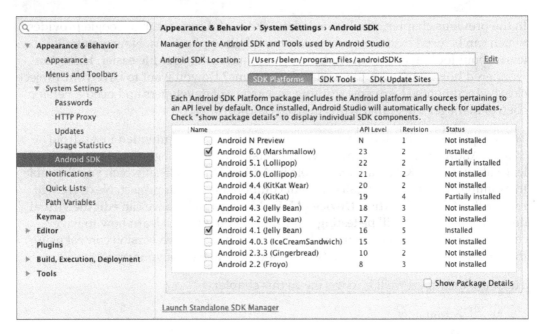

The SDK path configured in Android Studio is displayed at the top of the manager. You can change its path by clicking on the **Edit** button. The SDK Manager displays the list of available **SDK Platforms** packages with the following properties:

- **Name**: This is the name of the container that aggregates related packages. Check the **Show Package Details** checkbox under the list of packages to see the details of the container.

- **API level**: This is the API number in which the package was added.

- **Revision**: This is the package revision or version.

- **Status**: This is the status of the package on your system. The status can be *Not installed*, *Installed*, *Update available*, *Not compatible*, or *Obsolete*. If the **Show Package Details** checkbox is unchecked, then the status can also be *Partially installed*. With **Show Package Details** unchecked, a container package is considered *Installed* when both the **SDK Platform** and **Sources for Android SDK** packages are installed. If there is only one of these packages installed, the container package status is *Partially installed*.

In the SDK Tools tab, you can manage the available SDK developer tools such as **Android SDK Platform-tools**, **Android Support Library**, or **Google Play services**, which will be explained in *Chapter 7*, *Google Play Services*.

In the **SDK Update Sites** tab, we can examine the list of official sites that provide add-ons and extra packages. We can add our custom external sites using the **Add** button at the bottom of the list.

Click on the **Launch Standalone SDK Manager** button at the bottom of the screen to open the standalone SDK Manager. This manager was the only option available in old versions of Android Studio. From the standalone SDK Manager, the SDK platforms and tools are listed like in the integrated SDK Manager, but we can also find some more options to filter and select the packages.

The packages can be filtered by their state using the checkboxes under the list. These options are also accessible from the **Packages** menu at the top.

Next to the name of the packages, there is a checkbox to select the packages we want to install, update, or delete. As shown in the next screenshot, the packages that are installed in our system and also have an update available are checked by default:

Packages			
Name	API	Rev.	Status
Tools			
✓ Android SDK Tools		24.1.2	Update available: rev. 24.4.
✓ Android SDK Platform-tools		21	Update available: rev. 23.0.
Android SDK Build-tools		23.0.1	Not installed
Android SDK Build-tools		22.0.1	Not installed

If there is a new Android platform version that is not installed, its packages will also be checked, as shown in the following screenshot:

Packages			
Name	API	Rev.	Status
☐ ▸ ☐ Tools			
☐ ▸ ☐ Tools (Preview Channel)			
☑ ▾ ☐ Android N (API 23, N preview)			
☑ ☐ SDK Platform Android N Preview	N	1	☐ Not installed
☑ ☐ Android TV Intel x86 Atom System Image	N	1	☐ Not installed
☑ ☐ Intel x86 Atom_64 System Image	N	1	☐ Not installed
☑ ☐ Intel x86 Atom System Image	N	1	☐ Not installed

The total number of selected packages to be installed or updated is indicated in the text of the button at the bottom of the dialog. The button under it indicates the total number of selected packages to be deleted. You can delete packages that are deprecated or packages that you do not need anymore.

Check the packages that need to be updated and also check the last Android platform. In addition, you should check the minimum platform supported by our application (Android 4.1.2, API 16) to be able to test our application in a virtual device using this version. Click on the **Install** button.

In the next dialog, we have to accept the package licenses. Check the **Accept License** radio button and click on the **Install** button. The installation or update of the packages will start showing its progress. First, the manager downloads the packages, then it unzips them, and, finally, it installs them.

Remember to check the SDK Manager from time to time for updates.

The AVD Manager

The **AVD Manager** is an Android tool accessible from Android Studio to manage the Android virtual devices that will be executed in the Android emulator.

To open the AVD Manager from Android Studio, navigate to **Tools | Android | AVD Manager**. You can also click on the shortcut from the toolbar. The AVD Manager displays the list of the existing virtual devices. Since we have not created any virtual devices, the list will initially be empty. To create our first virtual device, click on the **Create Virtual Device** button to open the configuration dialog.

The first step is to select the hardware configuration of the virtual device. The device definitions are listed on the left-hand side of the window. Device definitions can be classified into one of these categories: **Phone**, **Tablet**, **Wear**, or **TV**. Select one of them in the **Phone** category, such as Nexus 6, to examine its details on the right-hand side, as shown in the following screenshot:

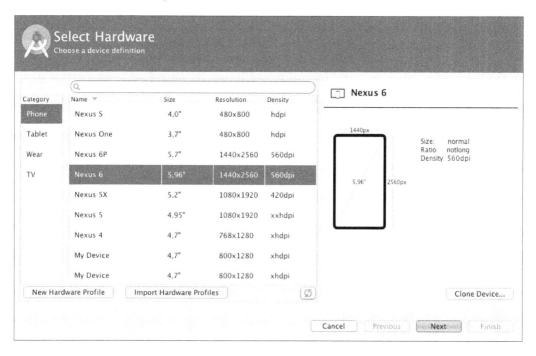

We can also configure our own hardware device definitions from the AVD Manager. We can create a new definition using the **New Hardware Profile** button. The **Clone Device...** button creates a duplicate of an existing device.

Click on the **New Hardware Profile** button to examine the existing configuration parameters. The parameters that define a device are:

- **Device Name**: This is the name of the device.
- **Device Type**: This is the device type, which can be a **Phone/Tablet**, **Android Wear**, or **Android TV**.

- **Screensize**: This is screen size in inches. This value determines the size category of the device. Type a value of 4.0 and notice how the **Size** value (on the right-hand side) becomes **normal**, as the following screenshot shows:

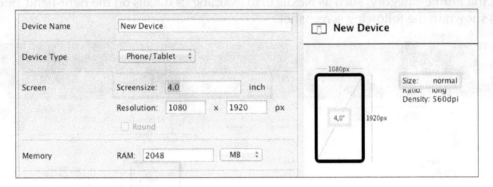

Now, type a value of 7.0 and the **Size** field changes its value to **large**, as the following screenshot shows:

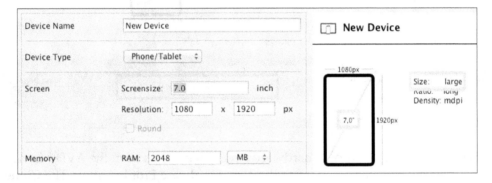

This parameter, along with the screen resolution, also determines the **Density** category.

- **Resolution**: This is the screen resolution in pixels. This value determines the density category of the device. For a screen size of 4.0 inches, type a value of 768 x 1280 and note how the **Density** value becomes **360 dpi**. Change the screen size to 6.0 inches and the **Density** value changes to **hdpi**. Now, change the resolution to 480 x 800 and the **Density** value will be **mdpi**.

- **RAM**: This is the RAM memory size of the device.

- **Input**: This configures software and hardware inputs. The **Has Hardware Buttons** checkbox indicates whether the **Back**, **Home**, or **Menu** buttons of the device are available via software or hardware. The **Has Hardware Keyboard** checkbox indicates whether the keyboard is available via software or hardware. The **Navigation Style** selector enables the navigation controls via Directional Pad (**D-Pad**), **Trackball**, or **Wheel**.

- **Supported device states**: This checks the allowed states, which are **Portrait** and **Landscape**.

- **Cameras**: This checks whether the device has a **Front-facing camera** or a **Back-facing camera**.

- **Sensors**: These are the sensors available in the device. They are **Accelerometer**, **Gyroscope**, **GPS**, and **Proximity Sensor**.

- **Default Skin**: This selects additional hardware controls.

Create a new device with a screen size of 5.5 inches, a resolution of 1080 x 1920, a RAM value of 2048 MiB, software buttons (leave input boxes unchecked), and both portrait and landscape states enabled. Name it `My Device`. Then, click on the **Finish** button. The hardware definition has been added to the list of configurations. If you right-click on the new hardware profile, you can edit it, clone it, export it, or delete it. Hardware profiles are exported using a XML format.

Click on the **Next** button to continue the creation of a new virtual device. The next step is to select the virtual device system image and the target Android platform. Each platform has its own architecture. The system images are listed on the left-hand panel and the details of a selected system image are shown in the right-hand panel. If a **Recommendation** message appears in the detail panel as shown in the next screenshot, follow the recommendation and select a different image.

Along with **Release Name** of a system image, there is a **Download** button. Select one of the **Recommended** images of the Marshmallow (API level 23) release with Google APIs and click on the **Download** button. Wait until the installation is finished and click on the **Next** button.

The last step is to verify the configuration of the virtual device. Enter the name of the AVD in the **AVD Name** field. Give the virtual device a meaningful name to recognize it easily, such as AVD_nexus6_api23. Click on the **Show Advanced Settings** button. The settings that we can configure for the virtual device are the following:

- **Startup size and orientation**: Select a scale for the screen and the initial orientation of the device. We recommend selecting the **Auto** scale.

- **Camera**: Select this if the emulator has a front camera or a back camera. The camera can be **Emulated** (which emulates that the device is actually capturing a video with the camera) or can be real (by the use of a **Webcam** from the computer).

- **Network**: Select the speed of the simulated network and the delay in processing data across the network. This is useful for testing your app with low connections or missing responses.

- **Emulated Performance**: Select how graphics are rendered in the device. They can be rendered using your computer's graphics (**Hardware**) or they can be emulated in software (**Software**). We recommend selecting the **Auto** option.

- **Memory and Storage**: Select the memory parameters of the virtual device. Leave the default values as they are, but, if a warning message is shown, follow the instructions of that message. For example, select **1536M** for the **RAM** memory and **64** for the **VM Heap**. The **Internal Storage** option can also be configured, for example, **200 MiB**. Select the size of **SD Card** or select a file to behave as the SD card.

- **Device Frame**: Select this if additional hardware controls are displayed in the emulator.

- **Keyboard**: Select this if a hardware keyboard is displayed in the emulator.

Click on **Finish**. The new virtual device is now listed in the AVD Manager. On the **Actions** section of the recently created virtual device, you can find the following actions:

- **Start** icon: This runs the virtual device.

- **Edit** icon: This edits the virtual device configuration.

- **Duplicate**: This creates a new device configuration displaying the last step of the creation process. You can change its configuration parameters and then verify the new device.

- **Wipe Data**: This removes the user files from the virtual device.
- **Show on Disk**: This opens the virtual device directory in your system.
- **View Details**: This opens a dialog detailing the virtual device's characteristics.
- **Delete**: This deletes the virtual device.
- **Stop**: This stops the virtual device.

A **Download** button in the **Actions** section, like in the next screenshot, means that the system image of that AVD is missing. Click on the **Download** button to install it in your system:

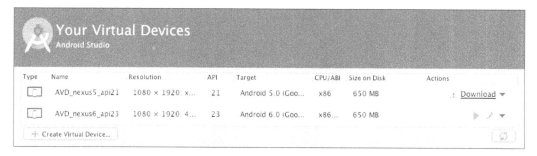

The recently created AVD will also be listed in the device selector of the graphical editor of a layout. In Android Studio, open the main layout with the graphical editor and click on the list of the devices. As the following screenshot shows, our custom device definition appears and we can select it to preview the layout:

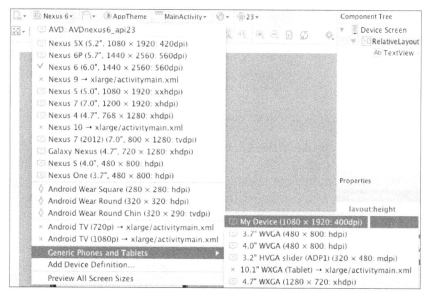

The Android emulator

Now that we have one AVD created in the AVD Manager, we can run it on the Android emulator. Open the AVD Manager and click on the **Start** button of the AVD. The emulator will be opened, as shown in the next screenshot. Wait until it is completely loaded and then you will be able to try it.

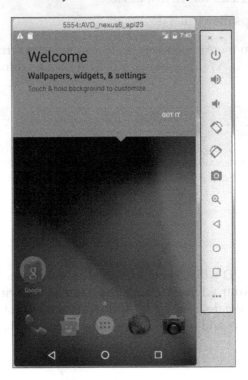

Next to the emulator, to its right-hand side, there is a bar with actions: power button, volume up and down, rotate left and right, take screenshot, zoom, back button, home button, overview button, and the extended controls.

Click on the **More** option to open the next extended controls:

- **Location**: This emulates the location of the device by setting latitude, longitude, and altitude. You can also emulate a series of location changes. Unfortunately, no map is provided to easily select a location, but you can use Google Maps to get the latitude and longitude of the locations you want to emulate. This mechanism is useful if your app displays a map or depends on the user's location to trigger a specific action. To try this feature, open the Google Maps app on the virtual device. Enter some coordinates in the **Extended controls** and click on **SEND**. Observe how Google Maps draws your location in the one you entered as the following screenshot shows:

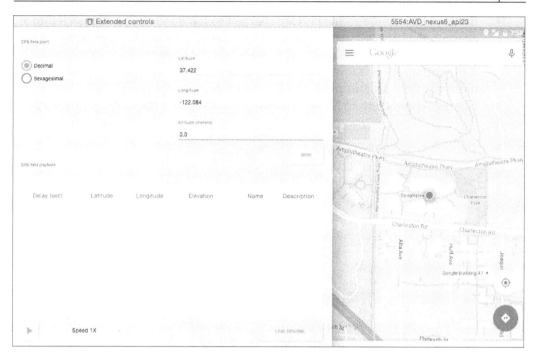

- **Cellular**: This emulates the speed of the network (**Full**, **HSDAP**, **UMTS**, and so on). This also emulates **Data status** and **Voice status**. This mechanism is useful, if your app depends on external data, to examine how it works with slow network connections. Try this feature by changing the **Network type** to **EDGE** and note how it changes in the emulator:

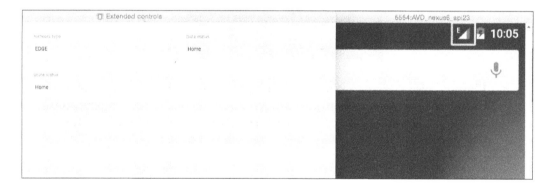

- **Battery**: This emulates the battery charge level, if the device is connected to a charger, the battery health, or the battery status. This mechanism is useful if your app changes its behavior depending on the battery status. For example, if the battery level is low, you can avoid unnecessary network requests to reduce battery consumption. If you change the **Charge level** to **10%** and the **Charger connection** to **None**, the emulator displays a low battery notification:

- **Phone**: This emulates a phone call or a SMS message. This mechanism is useful, for example, to examine how your app recovers from interruptions. To try this feature, click on the **CALL DEVICE** button and see how the device receives the call, as the next screenshot shows:

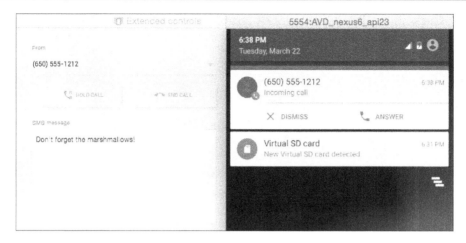

- **Directional pad**: This emulates a directional pad.

- **Fingerprint**: This emulates a finger touching the fingerprint sensor. This mechanism is useful if your app has a fingerprint security step, for example, to make a payment. To try this feature, open the Android **Settings** in the virtual device, go to **Security**, and click on **Fingerprint**. Follow the steps to add a fingerprint. You will get to the step, shown in the next screenshot, in which you need put your finger on the sensor:

Click on the **TOUCH SENSOR** button from the **Extended controls**. The fingerprint will be added as shown in the following screenshot:

Click on the power button to lock the device and click it again to unlock it. The fingerprint is then required. Click on the **TOUCH SENSOR** button using the same fingerprint and the device will be unlocked.

- **Settings**: These are the settings of the emulator. For example, you can change the folder to save the screenshots or if you want to send crash reports.
- **Help**: This contains **Keyboard shortcuts**, **Emulator help**, and **About**.

Finally, if you selected an emulated camera when you created the device definition, you can test it by opening the camera app in the emulator. Open it and note how a random video appears as if the camera was capturing it:

Generating Javadoc

Javadoc is a utility to document Java code in HTML format. The Javadoc documentation is generated from comments and tags added to Java classes or methods. The comments start with the /** string and end with */. Inside these comments, tags can be added. The following tags, in the same order as they should be added, are available in Javadoc:

- @author: This indicates the author or authors of the code.
- @version: This indicates the version of the class or method. Used for classes and interfaces.
- @param: This describes a method parameter. Only used in methods and constructors.
- @return: This describes the return object of a method. Only used in methods that do not return void.

- `@throws`: This describes an exception that can be thrown by the method. Equivalent to `@exception`.

- `@see`: This indicates a reference, which can be an URL, another element in the documentation, or just some text.

- `@serial`: This indicates if a field is serializable.

- `@deprecated`: This indicates that a method is deprecated and there is a replacement.

The use of Javadoc is integrated in Android Studio. We can use code completion when typing Javadoc comments. Javadoc documentation will appear in the pop-up tool tips of the code elements.

To generate a complete Javadoc, we have to write the Javadoc comments about our classes and methods. Open the main activity of our project to add the Javadoc comments to the `onAcceptClick` method we created in *Chapter 5, Creating User Interfaces*. Place the caret on the line before the method declaration, type `/**`, and press *Enter*. The Javadoc comments are automatically inserted containing the available information from the method declaration: parameters and return type. In this case, there is no return type, so the automatically generated Javadoc is the following:

```
/**
 *
 * @param v
 */
```

The first line of the documentation comments is the method description. Then, it explains each parameter and the return type. The method should now look like this:

```
/**
 * Method executed when the user clicks on the Accept button.
 * Change the greeting message to include the name introduced by
the user in the editText box.
 *
 * @param v View the user clicked
 */
public void onAcceptClick(View v) { ... }
```

This information about the method will now be displayed as its documentation in the emerging dialogs. The following screenshot shows the dialog that should appear over the method:

To generate the Javadoc documentation, navigate to **Tools | Generate Javadoc...**. A dialog showing the Javadoc options will be opened. We can select the scope, if we want to include test or library sources, the output directory, and the visibility of the included elements. Related to the format of documentation, we can create a hierarchy tree, a navigation bar, and an index if needed.

Check **Current File** as scope to generate just the documentation of our main activity. Select an output directory from your system. Reduce the visibility to **public** and click on the **OK** button. The Javadoc documentation in HTML format has been created in the output directory. The index.html file is the start point. Open the index.html file and navigate through the documentation to open the MyActivity class, like in the following screenshot. Note that the onCreate method, whose visibility is protected, does not appear, as we reduced the visibility of the generated Javadoc to **public** elements.

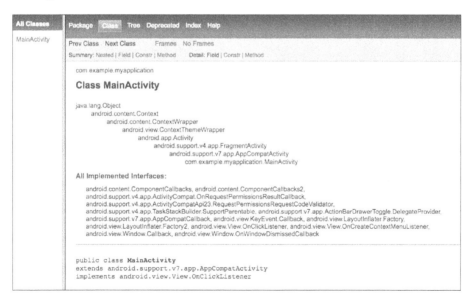

Tasks and contexts

Android Studio integrates several issue tracking systems. An issue tracking system is a software tool that manages lists of issues. Some issue tracking systems supported by Android Studio are the following: Jira, YouTrack, Lighthouse, Mantis, Trello, or Bugzilla.

To integrate one of these tracking systems into your project using Android Studio, navigate to **Tools | Tasks & Contexts | Configure Servers...**. Click on the **Add** button and select one of the available systems. You need to enter the server URL, the authentication values, and some additional parameters depending on the system type.

From the **Tasks & Contexts** menu you will find the actions to manage the tasks, such as switching among tasks, creating a new task, closing the current task, or editing the current task.

A task is identified by its name and is usually attached to an issue in your issue tracking system. A task can also be associated with a context, which defines a set of files that will be opened in the editor when you work on it. You can create, load, or clear a context from the **Tasks & Contexts** menu.

Let's create a task. Navigate to **Tools | Tasks & Contexts | + Open Task...**. Type the name, for example, `My first task`, and click on **Create New Task 'My first task'**. The creation dialog will be displayed as in the next screenshot:

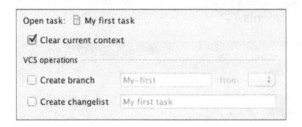

When you create a new task, you can clear the context and create a new branch in your VCS. Click **OK** to finish the creation. If you check the **Clear current context** option, all the files that were open in the editor are now closed.

In the toolbar of Android Studio there is a new item, a drop-down list with your tasks. As shown in the next screenshot, our current task is the recently created **My first task**. Note the existence of a previous task, the **Default task**:

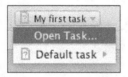

When you are ready to close a task, navigate to **Tools | Tasks & Contexts | Close Active Task...**. In the close task dialog, you can commit the changes and merge the current branch.

Version control systems

Android Studio integrates some **version control systems (VCS)**: GitHub, CVS, Git, Google Cloud, Mercurial, and Subversion. To enable version control integration, navigate to **VCS | Enable Version Control Integration...** and select the type of system. Now, some more options will be added to the **VCS** menu:

- To update the entire project, navigate to **VCS | Update Project...**
- To commit all the changes to the project, navigate to **VCS | Commit Changes...**

The first step is to do the checkout from the version control system. Navigate to **VCS | Checkout from Version Control**, click on the add icon, and type the repository URL or the repository configuration.

The version control actions can also be applied to individual files. Right-click on any file of the project and select the **Subversion** section. From the emerging menu, we can add the file to the repository, add it to the ignore list, browse the changes, revert the changes, or lock it.

A simpler way to control the file versions is using the **Local History** option. Open the main activity file in the editor and navigate to **VCS | Local History | Show History**. The file history dialog will be opened. On the left-hand side of the dialog, the available versions of the file are listed. Select an older version to compare it to the current version of the file. The differences between the older version and the current version are highlighted. Gray color is used to indicate a block of deleted code, blue color to highlight the text that has changed, and green color to indicate the newly inserted text. From the top icons, we can revert the changes and configure the whitespaces visualization. The following screenshot shows the comparison between two versions of our main activity. We can observe how the method we recently added — the `onAcceptClick` method — is highlighted in green:

We can also examine the local history of a specific block of code. Close the dialog, select some lines of code from the editor, and navigate to **VCS | Local History | Show History for Selection**. The same history dialog will be opened, but, this time, it displays the versions of the selected code.

Summary

By the end of this chapter, you have the knowledge required to use the Android SDK Manager tool to install, update, or examine available platforms for your project. You can create a new AVD and edit it whenever necessary. Creating complete documentation for our project should no longer be a problem using Javadoc and we should also be able to work with a VCS integrated in Android Studio.

In the next chapter, you will learn about the available Google Play services and how to integrate them with your project using Android Studio. We will also see how to install and integrate different libraries available with Google technology, such as Google Maps, Google Cloud Messaging, and more.

7
Google Play Services

Now that we have become familiar with the use of components on layouts, it is time to start thinking about extra functionality. Google Play services give you features, such as Google Maps, Google+, and more, to attract users. What are all the available features? How can you add these features to your application? What are the Android version requirements to use Google Play services?

This chapter focuses on the creation, integration, and use of Google Play services using Android Studio. You will learn what Google services are available. You will also learn about the standard authorization API that provides a safe way to grant and receive access tokens to Google Play services. Then, you will learn about the limitations of these services and also the benefits of using them.

These are the topics we'll be covering in this chapter:

- Existing Google Services
- Adding Google Play Services from the IDE
- Integrating Google Play Services in your app
- Understanding automatic updates
- Using Google services in your app

How Google Play services work

When Google previewed Google Play services at Google I/O 2012, it said that the platform "consists of a services component that runs on the device and a thin client library that you package with your app" (`https://developers.google.com/events/io/2012/`).

This means that Google Play services work thanks to two main components:

- **Google Play services client library**: The Google Play services client library includes interfaces to each Google service used by your app. The library is included when you pack your app and it allows your users to authorize the app with access to these services using their credentials. The client library is upgraded from time to time by Google, adding new features and services. You may upgrade the library in your app through an update to your app, although this is not necessary if you are not including any of the new features.

- **Google Play services APK**: The Google Play services APK runs as a background service in the Android operating system. Using the client library, your app accesses this service, which carries out the actions during runtime. The APK is not guaranteed to be installed on all devices. If the device does not come with the APK installed, you can get it from the Google Play store.

In this way, Google manages to separate the runtime of their services from the implementation you do as a developer, so you do not need to upgrade your application every time Google Play services are upgraded.

The Google Play services APK is automatically updated by the Google Play store. Any Android device running Android 2.3 or newer is ready to install any application that uses Google Play services.

Available services

Google Play services let you easily add more features to attract users on a wide range of devices, while using well-known features powered by Google. Using these services, you can add new revenue sources, manage the distribution of the app, access statistics, learn about your application users' habits, and improve your application with easy-to-implement Google features such as Maps or Google's social network, Google+. Some of the services are explained as follows:

- **Google+**: Using the Google+ Platform for Android, you can authenticate the user of your app. Once they are authenticated, you can also access their public profile and social graph, among other actions.

- **Google Analytics**: By integrating this service, you can allow your app to send information to Google Analytics. It is a tool that collects the metrics of your app. Metrics can help you to learn how users use your app by tracking events, like the number of taps on a button or by tracking the visualization of screens and components.

- **Google App Indexing**: By integrating this service, you can make the content of your app available to the Google app index. This will make your app easier for users to find.

- **Google Cast**: By integrating this service, you can make you app interact with Google Cast devices, such as Chromecast or Android TV.

- **Google Cloud Messaging**: Using **Google Cloud Messaging (GCM)** for Android, you can exchange data between the app running in an Android-based device and your server. Using GCM, your server can start the communication with your app, which can generate push notifications to the user.

- **Google Drive**: Using the Google Drive API, you can enable your application to access and manage your users' files stored in their Google Drive account.

- **Google Fit**: Using the Google Fit APIs, you can interact with **Bluetooth Low Energy (BLE)** devices (a heart rate monitor, a cycling sensor, or a pedometer), access data, or manage user activity in Google Fit.

- **Google In-app Billing**: Using Google Play In-app Billing makes it possible for you to sell digital content from your apps. You can use this service to sell one-time billing or temporal subscriptions to premium services and features.

- **Google Location**: By integrating the location APIs, you can make your application location aware.

- **Google Maps**: By integrating the Google Maps API, you can use the maps provided by Google in your app and customize them.

- **Google Mobile Ads**: Using the Google Mobile Ads API, you can add AdMob banner ads to your app.

- **Google Nearby**: By integrating the Google Nearby service, you can make your app interact with nearby devices and execute actions based on proximity.

- **Google Panorama Viewer**: By integrating this service, you can enable the user to see a 360-degree panorama picture.

- **Google Places**: By integrating the Google Places API, you can use the places information provided by Google in your app.

- **Google Play Game services**: Using the Google Play Game services, you can improve your gaming with a more social experience, such achievements, leaderboards, game gifts, or player stats.

- **Google Sign-In**: By integrating Google Sign-In, users can securely register into your app using their Google account.

- **Google Wallet**: By integrating Google Wallet, you can store objects such as gift cards or loyalty programs in the cloud and use them to pay in stores or online.

Adding Google Play services to Android Studio

The first thing we need to know is what we need to add to our Android Studio. You just learned that the APK is available in the Google Play store and it is the actual runtime of the services. We, as developers, only need this package in our testing device while debugging our application. What we need to add to Android Studio is the Google Play services client library.

This library has to be declared as a dependency to your application, so perform the following steps:

1. Open the `build.gradle` file for your application module (`/app/build.gradle`).

2. Add a new dependency to the build of your app by typing the following line inside the `dependencies` block:

    ```
    dependencies {
        ...
        compile 'com.google.android.gms:play-services:8.4.0'
    }
    ```

    The latest Google Play Services version is 8.4 (December 2015). When new updates of the library are published, you will need to update the version number in the `build.gradle` file.

3. Navigate to **Tools | Android | Sync Project with Gradle Files** to synchronize your project with the new dependency on Google Play services.

4. Finally, add it to the manifest file of your application inside the application block:

    ```
    <meta-data android:name="com.google.android.gms.version"
      android:value="@integer/google_play_services_version" />
    ```

    You should have the library inside the `build` folder of your application project at `app/build/intermediates/exploded-aar/com.google.android.gms/`, as shown in the following screenshot:

As you can notice both in the previous screenshot and in your project, all the Google Play services have been included: `play-services-ads`, `play-services-analytics`, `play-services-appindexing`, and so on. This could be completely unnecessary if you only need some of the services and you don't want to include all of them. Since Google Play services Version 6.5, you can add the services independently.

For example, if you only want to add the Google Maps and the Google Places APIs, replace the dependency that we had before in the `build.gradle` file with the following two dependencies:

```
dependencies {
    ...
    compile 'com.google.android.gms:play-services-maps:8.4.0'
    compile 'com.google.android.gms:play-services-location:8.4.0'
}
```

Navigate to **Tools | Android | Sync Project with Gradle Files** to synchronize your project. Inside the `build` folder of your application project at `app/build/intermediates/exploded-aar/com.google.android.gms/`, now you can only find the Google Maps and the Google Places APIs, as shown in the next screenshot:

If you still have all the `play-services` folders, clean the project by navigating to **Build | Clean Project**.

Although we recommend using Gradle dependencies to include the Google Play services in your app, there is another way to use them in your app. You can download and install the Google Play services library in our system. This library is distributed through the Android SDK Manager. Now, perform the following steps:

1. Navigate to **Tools | Android | SDK Manager**. Open the standalone SDK Manager. We can find Google Play services in the packages list under the `Extras` folder.

2. Select the **Google Play services** checkbox and click on the **Install 1 package...** button:

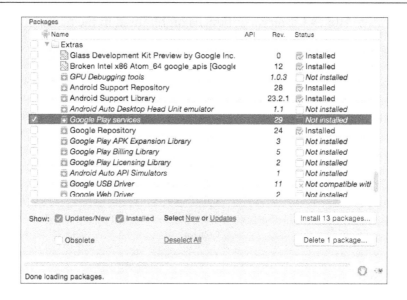

Performing these actions will add the library project into the location of our SDK installation folder, /sdk/extras/google/google_play_services/. You can check the exact path by hovering the mouse over the **Google Play services** row in the SDK manager and looking at the tool tip.

3. Navigate to the folder to examine its content. The samples folder contains some sample projects, for example, projects of Google Analytics (analytics/), authentication service (auth/), Google Cast (cast/), Google Drive (drive/), Google Maps (maps/), Google Panorama (panorama/), or Google Wallet (wallet/). The libproject/ folder contains the Google Play services library project. The google-play-services.jar file is placed in this folder at libproject/google-play-services_lib/libs/google-play-services.jar. The docs/ folder contains the documentation.

4. Add this JAR file to your project simply by dragging it into the libs/ folder.

5. Select the JAR file and right-click on it.

6. Select the **Add as Library...** option, as highlighted in the next screenshot:

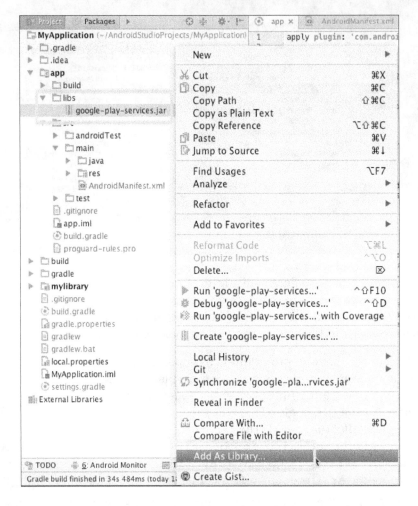

Select your application module in the **Create Library** dialog and click on **OK**. You now have the `google-play-services.jar` available in your project libraries, under the `libs/` folder, and you will now be able to reference Google Play services from your code.

7. Finally, you will need to add the library to your Gradle's build file. To do this, just edit the `build.gradle` file under `MyApplication/` and add the following line in the `dependencies` section:

```
dependencies {
    ...
    compile files('libs/google-play-services.jar')
}
```

Google Maps Android API

Google Maps Android API allows the users of your application to explore maps available through a Google service. It offers functionalities such as 3D maps, indoor and satellite maps, efficient caching and drawing using vector-based technology, and animated transitions through the map. Add the following dependency, to your Gradle's build file, to include the Google Maps API package in your app:

```
compile 'com.google.android.gms:play-services-maps:8.4.0'
```

Let's create a new activity, **Google Maps Activity**, to examine the most important generated classes. Navigate to **File | New | Activity | Gallery....** In the **Add an Activity to Mobile** dialog, select a **Google Maps Activity** and click on **Next**. In the **Customize the Activity** step, leave the default values like they are in the screenshot: `MapsActivity` for **Activity Name**, `activity_maps` for **Layout Name**, and `Map` for **Title**:

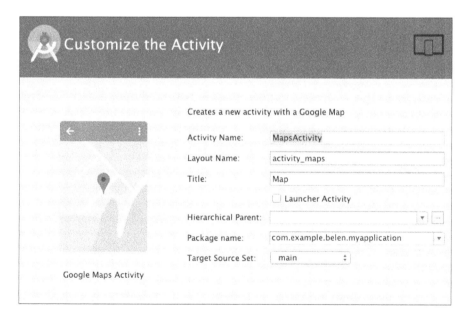

Click on **Finish**. Three new files were created: the activity `MapsActivity.java` (at `src/main/java`), the layout `activity_maps.xml` (at `src/main/res/layout`), and one resource file, `google_maps_api.xml` (at `/src/debug/res/values` and at `/src/release/res/values`). This resource file contains the Google Maps API Key that you need to be able to use the Google Maps API. Open the link provided in the resource file and follow the directions. Once you have created your key, paste it in the resource file, replacing the `YOUR_KEY_HERE` text.

Open the `MapsActivity` class under `src/main/java/`. Check the `import` clauses in the activity and notice that the `com.google.android.gms.maps` package contains the Google Maps Android API classes. The activity has a `private` variable of class type `GoogleMap`, which is the main class of the API, and this is the entry point for all the methods related to a map. You may change the theme colors and the icons of your map to match your application style. You can also customize your map by adding markers to it. To add a simple marker, you can use the `addMarker` method of the `GoogleMap` class. Examine the `onMapReady` method in `MapsActivity` to see the following code:

```
LatLng sydney = new LatLng(-34, 151);
mMap.addMarker(new MarkerOptions().position(sydney).title("Marker in
Sydney"));
```

The `addMarker` method has a `MarkerOptions` object as a parameter. Using the `position` method, we indicate the coordinates of the marker on the map and use the `title` method, we can add a custom string to show up on the marker.

To add a map into a layout, we can use the `MapView` class, which extends the `View` class and displays a map. However, the easiest way to place a map in an application is using a `MapFragment` object. A `fragment` represents a piece of the user interface or behavior that can be embedded in an activity. A `fragment` is a reusable module.

The `MapFragment` class wraps a view of a map to handle the necessary life cycle requirements of a component automatically. To see this code in use, open the layout associated with the `MapsActivity` class. This is the `activity_maps.xml` file found under `/res/layout/`. The `MapFragment` class extends the `Fragment` class, so it can be added to a layout by adding the following XML code:

```
<fragment
    android:id="@+id/map"
    android:name="com.google.android.gms.maps.SupportMapFragment"
    android:layout_width="match_parent"
    android:layout_height="match_parent" />
```

Finally, we need the code to obtain the `GoogleMap` object from the fragment. We can find the `Fragment` map using the `findFragmentById` method, and then we get the map from the `Fragment` using the `getMap` method:

```
MapFragment mapFragment = (MapFragment)
    getFragmentManager().findFragmentById(R.id.map);
```

You can see an example of this code in the `MapsActivity` class in the `onCreate` method.

The last important class to cover is the `GoogleMapOptions` class, which can be used if you create your map programmatically. It defines the configuration for a map. You can also modify the initial state of a map by editing the layout XML code or using the setters' methods of the map from your activity code. Here are some interesting options that are available:

- `mapType`: This specifies the type of a map. Its value can be `none`, `normal`, `hybrid`, `satellite`, or `terrain`.
- `compassEnabled`: This defines whether compass controls are enabled or disabled.
- `zoomControlsEnabled`: This defines whether zoom controls are enabled or disabled.
- `rotateGesturesEnabled`: This defines whether rotation gestures are enabled or disabled.

There are some sample demos at Google Map's GitHub: `https://github.com/googlemaps/android-samples`.

Google Places

Using the Google Places API, your app can access the Google's places database. This database has information about business and local places: name, address, photos, phone number, rating, type, coordinates, website, or price level. Add the following dependency in your Gradle's build file to include the Google Places API package in your app:

```
compile 'com.google.android.gms:play-services-location:8.4.0'
```

To use the Google Places API, an API key is needed. This key is the same one that you obtained to use the Google Maps API. Once you have it, add it to your app's manifest file, inside the `application` element, using the following code:

```
<meta-data
android:name="com.google.android.geo.API_KEY"
android:value="YOUR_API_KEY_HERE"/>
```

The `GoogleApiClient` class is used to access the API. Add the Google Places API in the `Build` method by indicating any of the two available Places API keys:

- **Geo Data API**: This API provides access to Google's database, which contains the information about local places and businesses. The key for this API is `Places.GEO_DATA_API`.

- **Place Detection API**: This API gets the device location and detects the nearby places. The key for this API is `Places.PLACE_DETECTION_API`.

You can also add both of them. See the following code as an example for the `onCreate` method of your activity:

```
GoogleApiClient gac = new GoogleApiClient
        .Builder(this)
        .addApi(Places.GEO_DATA_API)
        .addApi(Places.PLACE_DETECTION_API)
        .addConnectionCallbacks(this)
        .addOnConnectionFailedListener(this)
        .build();
```

In addition to these two APIs, there is a default dialog that your app can display to let the user pick a place in a map—the **Place Picker UI**. Using this element, you don't need to implement your own custom dialog. Use the `IntentBuilder` method of the `PlacePicker` class to create an `Intent` and start the activity like in the following code:

```
PlacePicker.IntentBuilder builder =
    new PlacePicker.IntentBuilder();
startActivityForResult(builder.build(this), PLACE_PICKER_REQUEST);
```

The activity's result will return you the place selected by the user, which you can obtain using the `getPlace` method of the `PlacePicker` class:

```
@Override
public void onActivityResult(int requestCode, int resultCode, Intenta
data) {
    if (requestCode == PLACE_PICKER_REQUEST) {
        if (resultCode == Activity.RESULT_OK) {
            Place place = PlacePicker.getPlace(data, getActivity());
        }
    }
}
```

Geo Data API

Using the Geo Data API, which is connected to Google's database, you can find places by their identifiers or by query, you can get photos of the places, or you can add new places. These are the main methods available in the GeoDataApi interface:

- addPlace: This method allows you to add a new place to Google's database. The place will be available for your app, but it needs to be reviewed before being added to Google's database. Information about the new place is included in an AddPlaceRequest object.

- getAutocompletePredictions: This method returns a list of places based on a query that looks for names and addresses of places. In addition to the search string, you can add more filters, such as latitude and longitude limits or a flag to return only businesses.

- getPlaceById: This method returns a list of Place objects with the indicated place IDs.

- getPlacePhotos: This method returns up to 10 photos of the place indicated by its ID.

Place Detection API

To get an estimation of the place where the user is located, you need to use the Place Detection API. The PlaceDetectionApi interface provides the getCurrentPlace method that returns a buffer (PlaceLikelihoodBuffer object) containing a list of candidate places and the associated likelihood of the user being in those places (PlaceLikelihood objects). A PlaceLikelihood object has two public methods:

- getLikelihood: This method returns a float value, which represents the likelihood with a value from 0.0 to 1.0. The higher the value, the higher the confidence that the user is at that candidate place.

- getPlace: This method returns the Place object, which contains all the information about the candidate place.

The getCurrentPlace method can receive a filter to refine the results (PlaceFilter object). You can filter the places that are currently open or not and you can filter by specific place identifiers.

To see more code and examples, check the sample demo at Google's GitHub: https://github.com/googlesamples/android-play-places.

Google Sign-In

Google Sign-In for Android lets the developer authenticate users using the same credentials they use on Google. Users will be able to sign in to your app using their Google credentials. Add the following dependency in your Gradle's build file to include the Google Sign-In package in your app:

```
compile 'com.google.android.gms:play-services-auth:8.4.0'
```

These are the main Google Sign-In API classes that you need to know about:

- `SignInButton`: This is the default Google Sign-In button. You need to add the default or a custom button to your app so the user can trigger the Sign-In flow. You can add the default button using this code in your layout file:

```
<com.google.android.gms.common.SignInButton
  android:id="@+id/sign_in_button"
  android:layout_width="wrap_content"
  android:layout_height="wrap_content" />
```

This default button can be customized in size and color depending on the scope. For example, you can choose among these size values, which you can compare in the next screenshot: `SignInButton.SIZE_ICON_ONLY`, `SignInButton.SIZE_STANDARD`, or `SignInButton.SIZE_WIDE`.

- `GoogleSignInOptions`: This class configures the Google Sign-In API options. You can request the user's ID and basic profile using the `GoogleSignInOptions.DEFAULT_SIGN_IN` option. You can also build a new option to request additional information such as the user's e-mail using the following code:

```
GoogleSignInOptions gsio = new
  GoogleSignInOptions.Builder(
      GoogleSignInOptions.DEFAULT_SIGN_IN)
  .requestEmail()
  .build();
```

- `GoogleApiClient`: This class is used to access the API. Add the Google Sign-In API in the `Build` method by indicating the `Auth.GOOGLE_SIGN_IN_API` key. The build method also receives a `GoogleSignInOptions` object. You can add the following code to the `onCreate` method of your activity to get a `GoogleApiClient` object:

```
GoogleApiClient gac = new GoogleApiClient.Builder(this)
    .enableAutoManage(this, this)
    .addApi(Auth.GOOGLE_SIGN_IN_API, gsio)
    .build();
```

To see more code and examples, check the sample demo at Google's GitHub: `https://github.com/googlesamples/google-services/tree/master/android/signin`.

Google+ Platform for Android

Google+ Platform for Android is now part of Google Sign-In. You need to add Google Sign-In to use Google+ in your app. This enables the use of the public profile and social graph to welcome the users by name, display their pictures, or connect with friends.

Create a `GoogleApiClient` object to access the API and use the Sign-In feature. Add the Google+ API by indicating the key `Plus.API` and these two scopes: `Scopes.PLUS_LOGIN` and `Scopes.PLUS_ME`, like in the following code:

```
GoogleApiClient gac = new GoogleApiClient.Builder(this)
        .enableAutoManage(this, this)
        .addApi(Plus.API)
        .addScope(Scopes.PLUS_LOGIN)
        .addScope(Scopes.PLUS_ME)
        .build();
```

The `PlusShare` class includes resources in posts shared on Google+. The `PlusOneButton` class implements a **+1** button to recommend a URL on Google+. The available sizes for the **+1** button are small, medium, tall, or standard. Add it to a layout using the following code:

```
<com.google.android.gms.plus.PlusOneButton
  android:layout_width="wrap_content"
  android:layout_height="wrap_content"
  plus:size="standard" />
```

To see more code and examples, check the sample demo at Google's GitHub: `https://github.com/googleplus/gplus-haiku-client-android`.

Google Play In-App Billing

In-app Billing allows you to sell virtual content from your apps. This virtual content could be paid content with a one-time billing or a time concession through subscriptions or fees. Using this service, you can allows you to charge for extra features and access to premium content.

Any app published in Google Play store can implement the In-app Billing API, since it only requires the same assets as publishing an app: a Google Play Developer Console account and a Google Wallet Merchant account.

Using the Google Play Developer Console, you can define your products, including the type, identification code (SKU), price, description, and more. Once you have your products defined, you can access this content from this application. When the user wants to buy this content, the following purchase flow will occur between your In-app billing application and Google Play:

1. Your app calls `isBillingSupported()` to Google Play to check if the In-app Billing version your are using is supported.

2. If the In-app Billing API version is supported, you may use `getPurchases()` to get a list of the SKUs of the purchased items. This list will be returned in a `Bundle` object.

3. You will probably want to inform your user of the available in-app purchases. To do this, your app may send a `getSkuDetails()` request, which will result in a list with the price, title, description, and more information available for the item being offered.

To see more code and examples, check the sample demo at Google's GitHub: `https://github.com/googlesamples/android-play-billing`.

Google Cloud Messaging

Google Cloud Messaging (GCM) for Android allows the communication between your server and your application using asynchronous messages. You need the client implementation in your Android app, but you also need the implementation in your server to send the messages and to store the client's data. You don't have to worry about handling low-level aspects of this communication, such as queuing and message construction. Using this service, you can easily implement a notification system for your application.

The following image shows how GCM works. The process involves three elements: your app, your server, and the GCM servers.

1. Your app first needs to register in GCM to get a registration ID, which identifies your app in a specific device.

2. Your app has to send the registration ID to your server so that it can be saved. This second step is necessary since your server needs to know the registration IDs of the user's device to send a message to your app in that device.

3. When your server wants to send a message, it will send it to the GCM servers, indicating the message information and the registration IDs of the devices that will receive the message.

4. Finally, GCM will send the message to your app in those devices.

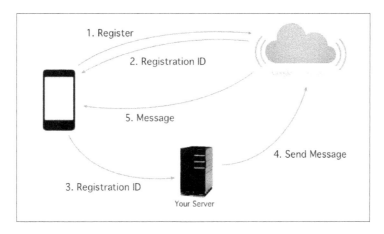

You have two options when using GCM:

- The server can inform your app when there is new data available to be fetched from the server, and then the application gets this data.

- The server can send the data directly in a message. The message payload can be up to 4 KB. This allows your application to access the data at once and act accordingly.

Add the following dependency, in your Gradle's build file, to include the Google Maps API package in your app:

```
compile 'com.google.android.gms:play-services-gcm:8.4.0'
```

In order to send or receive messages from your app (client side), you will need to get a registration ID. This identifies the combination of device and application. To allow your app to use the GCM service, you need to add the following line to the manifest file of your project:

```
<uses-permission
android:name="com.google.android.c2dm.permission.RECEIVE"/>
```

You also have to add the declaration of the following three classes to your manifest file:

- **GCM Receiver**: This class manages the messages received in your app. This receiver already belongs to the GCM API and you don't need to create it. Use the following code to add it to your manifest file:

```
<receiver
android:name="com.google.android.gms.gcm.GcmReceiver"
android:exported="true"
android:permission="com.google.android.c2dm.permission.SEND">
    <intent-filter>
        <action
        android:name="com.google.android.c2dm.intent.RECEIVE" />
        <category android:name="com.example.gcm" />
    </intent-filter>
</receiver>
```

- **GCM Listener Service**: This service class, which you have to create in your app, should extend the GcmListenerService class. By implementing this service subclass, you can handle the messages in its onMessageReceived method. Use the following code to add it to your manifest file:

```
<service
android:name="com.example.MyGcmListenerService"
android:exported="false" >
    <intent-filter>
        <action
        android:name="com.google.android.c2dm.intent.RECEIVE" />
    </intent-filter>
</service>
```

- **Instance ID Listener Service**: This service class, which you have to create in your app, should extend the `InstanceIDListenerService` class. By implementing this service subclass, you can handle the registration ID. Use the following code to add it to your manifest file:

```
<service
android:name="com.example.MyInstanceIDListenerService"
android:exported="false">
    <intent-filter>
        <action
        android:name="com.google.android.gms.iid.InstanceID" />
    </intent-filter>
</service>
```

To see more code and examples, check the sample demo at Google's GitHub: `https://github.com/googlesamples/google-services/tree/master/android/gcm`.

More sample apps

If you are interested in Google Play services, there are sample apps available at Google's GitHub. Here are the links to them:

- Google+: `https://github.com/googleplus/gplus-haiku-client-android`.

- Google Analytics: `https://github.com/googlesamples/google-services/tree/master/android/analytics`.

- Google App Indexing: `https://github.com/googlesamples/google-services/tree/master/android/app-indexing`.

- Google Cast: `https://github.com/googlecast/CastVideos-android` or `https://github.com/googlecast/GameManagerSamples`.

- Google Cloud Messaging: `https://github.com/googlesamples/google-services/tree/master/android/gcm`.

- Google Drive: `https://github.com/googledrive/android-demos`.

- Google Fit: `https://github.com/googlesamples/android-fit`.

- Google In-app Billing: `https://github.com/googlesamples/android-play-billing`.

- Google Location: `https://github.com/googlesamples/android-play-location/`.

- **Google Maps:** `https://github.com/googlemaps/android-samples`.

- **Google Mobile Ads:** `https://github.com/googlesamples/google-services/tree/master/android/admob`.

- **Google Nearby:** `https://github.com/googlesamples/android-nearby`.

- **Google Places:** `https://github.com/googlesamples/android-play-places`.

- **Google Play Games services:** `https://github.com/playgameservices/android-basic-samples`.

- **Google Sign-In:** `https://github.com/googlesamples/google-services/tree/master/android/signin`.

- **Google Wallet:** `https://github.com/android-pay/androidpay-quickstart`.

Summary

In this chapter, we discussed the available Google Play services. You learned how to improve our application using Google Play Services through its client library and Android package. You should have successfully installed the Google Play Services client library in Android Studio using the SDK Manager and should now be able to build applications using the library features. You also learned some tips about Google Maps v2, Google+ Platform for Android authentication, Google Play In-app Billing, and GCM.

In the next chapter, you will learn about some useful tools available in Android Studio. We will use the SDK Manager frequently to install different packages. You will also learn about the AVD Manager for different virtual devices to test our applications on. We will generate Javadoc documentation for our project using the Javadoc utility and you will learn about the version control systems available in Android Studio.

8
Debugging

The debugging environment is one of the most important features of an IDE. Using a debugging tool allows you to easily optimize your application and improve its performance. Do you want to use a debug tool while programming in Android Studio? Android Studio includes the **Dalvik Debug Monitor Server** (**DDMS**) debugging tool.

In this chapter, you will start by learning about the **run** and **debug** options and how to emulate your application in one of the Android virtual devices you learned to create in a previous chapter. You will learn about the **Debugger**, **Console**, and **LogCat** tabs in depth. You will also learn how to use breakpoints when using the debugger. We will end this chapter with information about each tab available in the advanced debugger tool included in Android Studio DDMS and the Hierarchy View.

These are the topics we'll be covering in this chapter:

- Debugging
- LogCat
- Instant run
- Device Monitor tools
- Hierarchy View

Running and debugging

Android applications can be run from Android Studio in a real device using a USB connection or in a virtual device using the emulator. Virtual devices make it possible to test our applications on different types of hardware and software configurations. In this chapter, we will use the emulator to run and debug our application because of its simplicity and flexibility.

To run an application directly, navigate to **Run | Run 'app'**. You can also click on the play icon from the toolbar. To debug an application, navigate to **Run | Debug 'app'** or click on the bug icon from the toolbar. If your app is already running, you can start the debug mode by navigating to **Run | Attach debugger to Android process**.

When we select the **Debug 'app'** option, a dialog to choose the device is opened. The **Connected Devices** section is used to choose a running device; the current connected devices are listed, real or virtual. The **Available Emulators** section is used to launch a new instance of the emulator; the available virtual devices are listed. You can also create a new emulator from this dialog using the **Create New Emulator** button. This option will open the virtual device configuration dialog that was explained in *Chapter 6, Tools*. One last option in this dialog is the **Use same selection for future launches** checkbox. Check this if you want to skip this step in future.

Select the virtual device created in *Chapter 6, Tools*, from the **Available Emulators** section as shown in the following screenshot and click **OK**.

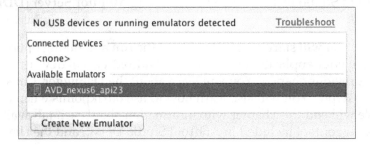

The emulator will be launched. The next time we run or debug the application, the emulator will be running, so we will select it from the **Connected Devices** section.

While debugging, you will note that, at the bottom of Android Studio as shown in the next screenshot, there is a new panel, **Debug**, which contains two tabs: **Debugger** and **Console**. The **Android Monitor** tab contains two other tools: **LogCat** and **Monitors**.

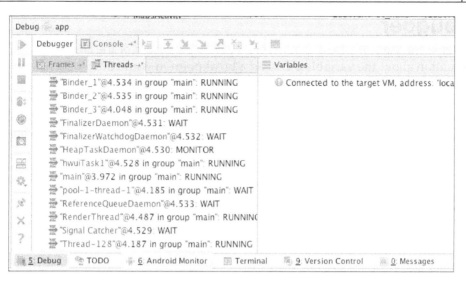

Console

Console displays the events that are taking place while the emulator is being launched or while it is running. Open it to examine the messages and check that the emulator and the application are being correctly executed. The actions that should appear are:

- **Waiting for device**: This is the starting point when the emulator is being launched.
- **Uploading file** (the `adb push` command): This event states that the application is packed and stored in the device.
- **Installing** (the `adb shell pm` install command): This event states that the application is being installed in the device. After the installation, a success message should be printed.
- **Launching application** (the `adb shell am start` command): This event takes place when the application starts to execute.
- **Waiting for process**: This event takes place when the application is running and the debug system tries to connect to the application process in the device.

After the success of the previous steps, the application will be visible in the emulator. Test it by typing any name in the text input and clicking on the **Accept** button. The greeting message should change.

Debugger

Debugger manages the breakpoints, controls the execution of the code, and shows information about the variables. To add a breakpoint in your code, just click on the left edge of a line of code. A red point will appear next to the line of code to indicate the breakpoint. To delete the breakpoint, click on it. If you right-click on a breakpoint, more options become available in a small dialog, in which you can click on the **More to open the Breakpoints** window, which is shown in the following screenshot:

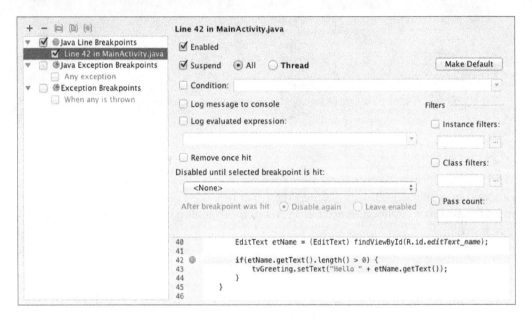

You can also open the **Breakpoints** window by navigating to **Run | View Breakpoints....** In the left-side panel of the **Breakpoints** window, all the breakpoints of your app are listed. You can add new breakpoints, remove them, or enable and disable them. You can enable **Exception Breakpoints**, which will be triggered when an exception is thrown while your app is running. If you select one breakpoint from the left-side panel, you can configure it using the right-side panel. For example, you can set a condition for the breakpoint, log a message to console, or remove it once it is hit.

Add a breakpoint in the conditional statement of the onAcceptClick method of our main activity and debug the application again, as shown:

```
c  MainActivity.java ×
33
34        /**...*/
38        public void onAcceptClick(View v) {
39            TextView tvGreeting = (TextView) findViewById(R.id.textView);
40            EditText etName = (EditText) findViewById(R.id.editText_name);
41
42 ○        if(etName.getText().length() > 0) {
43            tvGreeting.setText("Hello " + etName.getText());
44        }
45    }
46
```

Enter your name in the application and click on the **Accept** button. When the execution gets to the breakpoint, it pauses, and the **Debugger** tab is opened. Since we added the breakpoint in the conditional statement before assigning the text, our greeting message has not changed.

From the debugger tab, we can examine the method call hierarchy and the state of the variables at that point of execution. The available variables are the parameter of the v method, the TextView and EditText objects obtained by the findViewById method, and the reference to the current activity (this). Expand the EditText object named etName, as shown in the following screenshot, and search for the mText property. This property should contain the name you typed before:

Right-click on the EditText object to open a menu with more options and select **Evaluate Expression....** The **Evaluate Expression** dialog allows you to query methods in the context of the selected object. For example, type etName.getText() and press *Enter* to evaluate the expression. The result of the expression will be displayed like in the following screenshot:

When the execution of your app is stopped in a breakpoint, you can do the following actions:

- To execute the next line of code without stepping into the method call, you can navigate to **Run | Step Over**, click on the button in the top toolbar of the **Debug** panel, or press the keyboard shortcut indicated for this option, usually the *F8* key.

- To step into the method call, you can navigate to **Run | Step Into**, click on the button in the top toolbar of the **Debug** panel, or press *F7*.

- To choose the method you want to step into, navigate to **Run | Smart Step Into** or press *Shift +F7*.

- To step to the cursor position in your code, you can navigate to **Run | Run to Cursor**, click on the button in the top toolbar of the **Debug** panel, or press *Alt + F9*.

- To resume the execution until the next breakpoint, you can navigate to **Run | Resume Program**, click on the button in the left-side toolbar of the **Debug** panel, or press *F9*.

- To stop the execution, you can navigate to **Run | Stop**, click on the button in left-side toolbar of the **Debug** panel, or press *Ctrl + F2* (*Cmd + F2* on OS X).

These options, among others, are also available from the debugger tab as icon shortcuts.

Expand the `tvGreeting` object to check the value of its `mText` property. Now, step over the conditional statement and the call of the `setText` method. Note how the value of the `mText` property has changed, which is shown in the next screenshot. Finally, resume the execution so the greeting message changes in the device screen.

Create a new breakpoint inside the `if` clause. We can add a condition to the endpoint so the execution is only paused when the name typed by the user is `"no name"`, otherwise, the execution will continue as usual. The following screenshot of the **Breakpoints** window shows the breakpoint details:

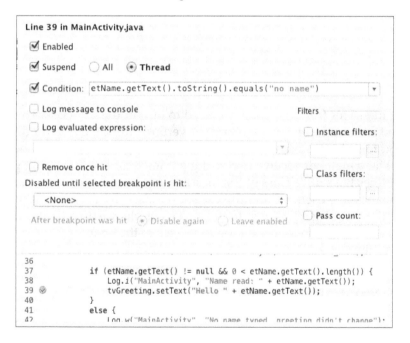

In the **Condition** field of the breakpoint, add the following condition that compares the text typed by the user in the name field (`etName`):

```
etName.getText().toString().equals("no name")
```

Now, if you write your name in the app, no breakpoint will suspend the execution. If you type `"no name"`, execution will be suspended at the recently created breakpoint.

LogCat

LogCat is the Android logging system that displays all the log messages generated by the Android system in the running device. Log messages have several levels of significance. From the **LogCat** tab, we can filter the log messages by these levels. For example, if we select the information level as the filter, the messages from **information**, **warning**, and **error** levels will be displayed. The levels are shown in the following diagram:

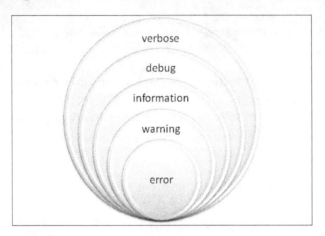

To print log messages from our code, we need to import the Log class. This class has a method for each level: the v method for verbose, the d method for debug, the i method for information, the w method for warning, and the e method for the error level. These methods receive two string parameters. The first string parameter usually identifies the source class of the message and the second string parameter identifies the message itself. To identify the source class, we recommend using a constant, static string tag. However, in the next example, we directly use the string to simplify the code. Add the following log messages to the onAcceptClick method of our main activity:

```
if(etName.getText().length() > 0) {
    Log.i("MainActivity", "Name read: " + etName.getText());
    tvGreeting.setText("Hello " + etName.getText());
}
else {
    Log.w("MainActivity", "No name typed, greeting didn't change");
}
```

We have a log message to inform us about the name obtained from the user input and a log message to print a warning if the user did not type a name. Remove any breakpoint we previously created and then debug the application.

The **LogCat** tab in the **Android Monitor** has by default printed the log messages generated by the current application. Reading the messages of your application can sometimes be complex and you need to filter the messages. In the **LogCat** tab, there is an expandable list where you can filter the log messages by their level of significance. You can also use the search field to look for certain log messages. There is another expandable list to configure some extra filters: the **No Filters** option displays all the logs generated by the device; the **Show only selected application** option displays the logs generated only by your app; and the **Edit Filter Configuration** option allows you to create a more complex filter. Select **Edit Filter Configuration** to examine this option. A dialog to create filters is opened as shown in the next screenshot:

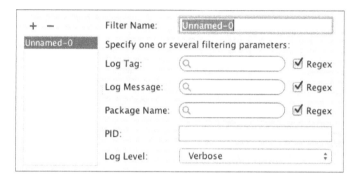

Log messages can be filtered using regular expressions by their **Log Tag**, their **Log Message**, or by the name of the package that printed them. Logs can also be filtered by the **process ID (PID)** or by their level.

Create a new filter named `MyApplication`, filter it by **Package Name** writing `com.example.myapplication` (our application package name), and click on **OK**. Now, the **LogCat** log has been filtered and it is easier to read our messages. Now, perform the following steps:

1. Focus on the **Emulator** window, enter a name in the application, and click on **Accept**. Observe how our log message is printed in the **LogCat** view.

2. Delete your name from the application and click on **Accept**. This time, a warning message is printed. Notice the different colors used for each type of message.

Monitors

The **Monitors** panel is available at the bottom-right corner of Android Studio. Select the device or emulator running your application, and select the process corresponding to your application from the two top expandable lists. There are four monitors available:

- **Memory**: This shows the free and allocated memory of the selected application over time, as shown in the following screenshot:

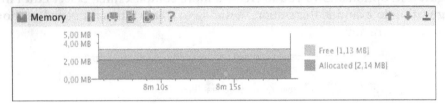

- **CPU**: This shows the CPU usage in real time of your app, as shown in the following screenshot:

- **Network**: This shows the network usage of your app, as shown in the following screenshot:

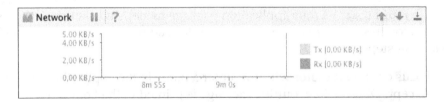

- **GPU**: This shows the GPU usage of your app, indicating the time to execute, process, prepare, and draw the frames, as shown in the following screenshot:

Instant run

Instant run is a new feature introduced in Android Studio 2.0 that allows you to update your app while it is running on a device without building a new APK. This feature reduces deployment time.

Instant run requires SDK 15 or higher, though it's recommended to use SDK 21 or higher. You will also need to have your Android Plugin for Gradle updated to version 2.0 or higher. Instant run works for both the emulator and a real device.

After the first deployment of your app, you will note that the run/debug icon has changed and has an additional thunderbolt icon, such as the debug icon in the following screenshot:

The next time you click on the **Debug** button, Android Studio will analyze the changes in your code to make the deployment of your app faster, instead of creating a new APK and doing a full deployment. There are three types of updates depending on the code that needs to be pushed to the app:

- **Hot swap**: This is the fastest swap. This type of swap is done if you change the code of an existing method. Android Studio will create a stub method with the new code and restart the current activity.

  If you do not want Android Studio to restart the current activity after a hot swap, you can disable this behavior in the settings screen. Instant run settings are in the **Build, Execution, Deployment** section of the main settings. The following screenshot shows the instant run settings screen:

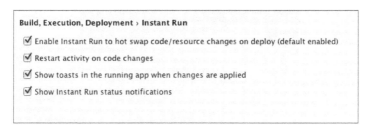

  You can disable the restart of the activity by disabling the **Restart activity on code changes** option.

- **Warm swap**: This type of swap is done if you change or remove an existing resource. Android Studio will always restart the current activity and you can't disable this behavior.

- **Cold swap**: This is the slowest swap and it requires API 21 or higher. If the device runs an API lower than 21, Android Studio will create a new APK and perform a full deployment. This type of swap is done if changes in the code are structural, such as changing the parent class, the implemented interfaces, a field, or a method signature. Android Studio will restart your app in a cold swap.

Android Studio will deploy a new build if you change the app manifest or anything that affects the app manifest, such as a resource referenced in the manifest.

Change some code in your app, for example, change the `Hello` text message to a `Goodbye` message:

```
tvGreeting.setText("Goodbye " + etName.getText());
```

Click on the **Debug** button with the thunderbolt. Since you changed the code in a method, Android Studio will do a hot swap. You will notice a flicker while the current activity restarts.

When the hot swap is finished, a message is displayed in the bottom part of Android Studio, as you can see in the next screenshot:

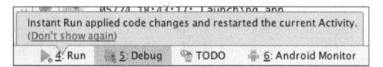

As you can read in the message, the code changes were applied and the current activity was restarted. Type a name and click on ACCEPT. The text message is the `Goodbye` one:

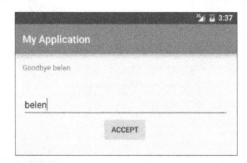

Disable the **Restart activity on code changes** option from the settings to observe the differences. Change the code back to the `Hello` text message and debug the app. There is no flicker now and, when the hot swap is finished, the message displayed in Android Studio is now different:

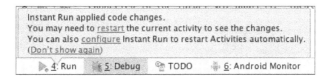

When the hot swap is finished, a message is also displayed in the emulator, like in the following screenshot. In this case, the message shown is: *Applied code changes without activity restart.*

Now change a resource, for example, change the hint of the `EditText` to the following one:

```
android:hint="Please, enter your name"
```

Click on the **Debug** button with the thunderbolt. Since you changed a resource, Android Studio will do a warm swap this time. You will notice that the current activity restarts again. The same message displays in the bottom part of Android Studio:

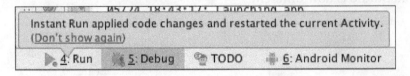

If you want to disable instant run completely, you can do it from the settings screen by unmarking the **Enable Instant Run to hot swap code/resource changes on deploy (default enabled)** option.

Android Device Monitor

The DDMS is a more advanced debugging tool available in the SDK. The DDMS can be accessed from Android Studio through the **Android Device Monitor** tool. This tool is able to monitor both a real device and the emulator.

To open the DDMS perspective, navigate to **Tools | Android | Android Device Monitor**. You can also click on the Android Device Monitor icon from the toolbar. A new window will be opened with the DDMS perspective.

In the left part of the window, the list of connected devices is shown. Currently, just our virtual device is listed. In the **Devices** section, the list of the processes running on each device is also presented. We should be able to locate our application in the processes of the device we launched before. From the toolbar of the **Devices** section, we can stop a process using the Stop sign icon. We can also take a screen capture of the virtual device by clicking on the Camera icon. Some of the other options will be explained later.

In the right part of the window, detailed information about the device is provided. This information is divided into seven tabs: **Threads, Heap, Allocation Tracker, Network Statistics, File Explorer, Emulator Control**, and **System Information**. **LogCat**, which has also been integrated in the DDMS perspective, is placed at the bottom part of the window.

Threads

The **Threads** tab displays the list of threads that belong to the selected process. Select our application process from the **Devices** section. The process is identified by the package name, in this case `com.example.myapplication`, click on the **Update Threads** icon button from the toolbar of the **Devices** section and the threads will be loaded in the content of the tab:

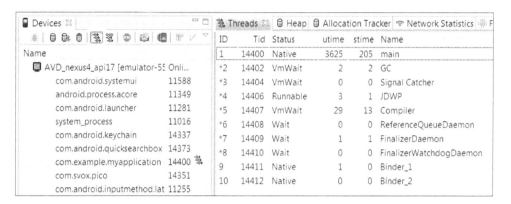

The first columns are the IDs of the threads. The **Status** column indicates the thread state, **utime** indicates the total time spent by the thread executing the user code, **stime** indicates the total time spent by the thread executing system code, and **Name** indicates the name of the thread. The threads that interest us are those that spend time executing our user code.

This **Threads** tool is useful if we create threads in our application apart from the main thread. We can check if they are being executed at a certain point of the application and whether their execution time is moderate or not.

Method profiling

Method profiling is a tool to measure the performance of methods execution in the selected process. The measured parameters are the number of calls and the CPU time spent while executing. There are the following two types of spent time:

- **Exclusive time**: This is the time spent in the execution of a method.
- **Inclusive time**: This is the total time spent on the execution of a method. This measure includes the time spent by any called methods inside the method. These called functions are known as its **children methods**.

To collect the method profiling data, select our application process from the **Devices** section and click on the **Start Method Profiling** icon from the toolbar of the **Devices** section, next to the **Update Threads** icon. A dialog to select the profiling option that you prefer is displayed. **Sample based profiling** profiles with less runtime performance impact using a sampling frequency, which can be configured. Sample-based profiling is available in Android 4.4 and later. **Trace based profiling** profiles the entry and exit of all the methods.

Perform some actions in the application; for example, in our example application, type a name and click on the **Accept** button in order to execute the onAcceptClick method of the main activity. Stop the method profiling by clicking on the **Stop Method Profiling** icon button.

When the method profiling is stopped, a new tab with the resultant trace is opened in the DDMS perspective. On the top of this new tab, the method calls are represented in a time graph; each row belongs to a thread. On the bottom of the trace, the summary of the time spent in a method is represented in a table.

Order the methods by their name to search for our onAcceptClick method (com.example.myapplication.MainActivity.onAcceptClick). Click on it to expand the detailed information about its execution. Now, note the following facts:

- The children methods called inside the onAcceptClick method are listed. We can see the EditText.getText method, the Activity.findViewById method, and the TextView.setText method, which we indeed directly call inside the method, as shown in the next screenshot.

- The number of calls is detailed in the **Calls/Total** column. For example, we can see that the Activity.findViewById method is called twice (**2/2** value) — one call to find the TextView object and a second call to find the EditText object.

- The **Exclusive time** columns have no values for the parent or children methods due to their own definition of this type of measured time:

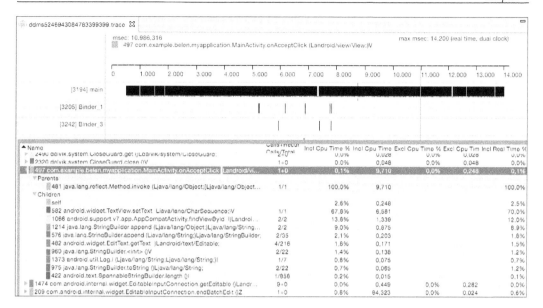

Method profiling is very useful to detect methods that spend too much time on their execution and to subsequently optimize them. We can identify the most expensive methods to avoid unnecessary calls to them.

Heap

The **Heap** tab displays the heap memory usage information and the statistics of the selected process. Select the application process and click on the **Update Heap** icon button from the toolbar of the **Devices** section to enable it. The heap information is shown after a **garbage collector** (GC) execution. To force it, click on the **Cause GC** button or the garbage icon from the toolbar of the **Devices** section.

The first table displays the summary of the heap usage: the total size, the allocated space, the free space, and the number of allocated objects. The **Stats** table gives the following detail of the objects allocated in the heap by type: the number of objects (**Count** column), the total size of those objects (**Total Size** column), the size of the smallest (**Smallest** column) and largest objects (**Largest** column), the median size (**Median** column), and the average size (**Average** column). Select one of the types to load the bottom bar graph.

The graph shows the count of the objects of a type by size, in bytes. If we right-click on the graph, we can change its properties (title, colors, font, labels, and so on) and save it as an image in the PNG format:

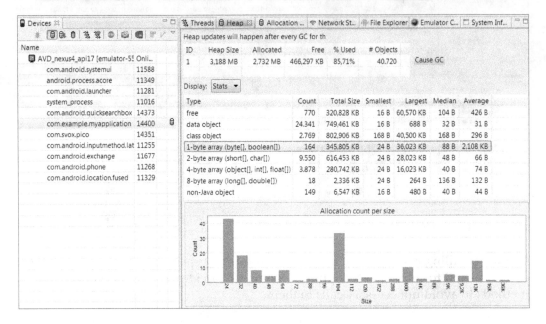

Allocation Tracker

The **Allocation Tracker** tab displays the memory allocations of the selected process. Select the application process and click on the **Start Tracking** button to start tracking the memory information. Then, click on the **Get Allocations** button to get the list of allocated objects.

We can use the filter on the top of the tab to filter the objects allocated in our own classes. Type our package name `com.example.myapplication` in the filter. For each object, the table shows its allocation size (**Allocation Size**), the thread (**Thread**), the object or class (**Allocated Class**), and the method in which the object was allocated (**Allocated in**). Click on any object to see more information, for example, the line number that allocated it.

As you can see in the next screenshot, a `java.lang.StringBuilder` object was allocated in the `onAcceptClick` of the main activity. In the bottom part, you can check the details of its allocation:

Finally, click on the **Stop Tracking** button.

The allocation tracker is very useful to examine the objects that are being allocated when doing certain interactions in our application, in order to improve memory usage.

Network Statistics

The **Network Statistics** tab displays how our application uses the network's resources. To get the network statistics of any application that uses the network, click on the **Start** button. The data transfers will begin to appear in the graph.

The network statistics are useful to optimize the network requests in our code and control the data transferred at a certain point of the execution.

File Explorer

The **File Explorer** tab exposes the whole filesystem of the device. We can examine the size, date, or permissions of each element. Navigate to `/data/app/` to search for our `com.example.myapplication.apk` application package file.

Emulator Control

The **Emulator Control** tab allows us to emulate some special states or activities in the virtual device. We can test our application in different environments and situations to check whether it behaves as expected. If our application has features that depend on the device's physical location, we can use mock locations. Some of these special states are:

- **Telephony Status**: This allows you to choose the voice and data status and its speed and latency
- **Telephony Actions**: This is used to simulate an incoming call or SMS
- **Location Controls**: This is used to set the geolocation of the device

System Information

The **System Information** tab presents the frame render time, total CPU load, and total memory usage of the device as graphs. We can search for our application and easily compare it with the rest of the processes running on the device.

We can change the properties of the graphs such as colors, font, and title and we can save them as images in PNG format. To open these options, right-click on the graph elements.

Open the CPU load and save the graph while our application is running in the foreground. Then, close the application and update the CPU load by clicking on the **Update from Device** button. Note the difference between both graphs and the growth of the idle percentage, as shown in the following screenshot:

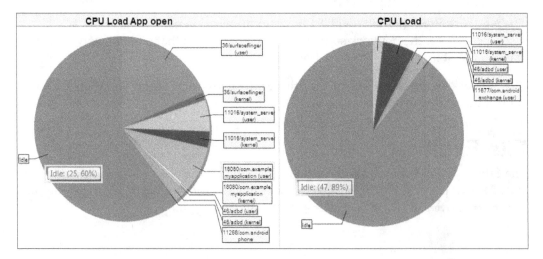

Hierarchy View

Android Device Monitor contains a second perspective apart from the DDMS—the **Hierarchy View**. On the top bar of the Android Device, you can change from one perspective to the other. The two options in the top bar are shown in the next screenshot:

Open the **Hierarchy View** perspective and select your app from the left-side list. In the left-side panel, click on the following icon (the **Load the view hierarchy into the tree view** action):

The view hierarchy is loaded as shown in the next screenshot:

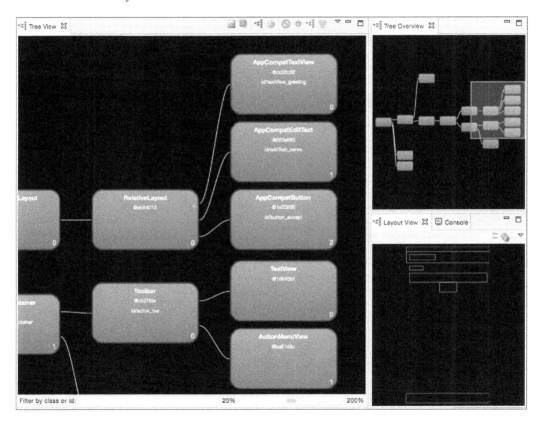

There are three different panels:

- **Tree Overview**: This panel shows the overview of the complete view hierarchy.

- **Tree View**: This panel shows in detail a specific area of the view hierarchy. At the bottom of the hierarchy, we can find the `TextView` with the ID `textView_ greeting`, the `EditText` with the ID `editText_name`, and the `Button` with the ID `button_accept`. The parent of all of them is the `RelativeLayout`.

- **Layout View**: This panel shows the layout view.

If you select one of the view elements, you can see its details. The following screenshot shows the details of the `button_accept` button:

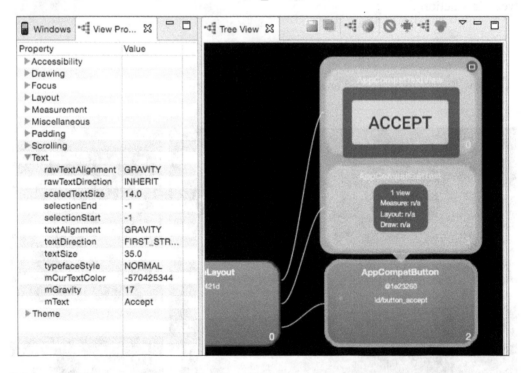

Open the **View Properties** tab from the left-side panel. You can check the properties of the button, such as the `mText` property, the value of which is `Accept`.

On the top of the **Tree View** panel, there are some actions like saving the tree view as a PNG image or capturing the window layers as a Photoshop file.

Summary

Now you know the different launch options for your application as well as how to use the console and the **LogCat** for debugging. We also saw how to debug an application and interpret the data provided by the DDMS in each of the tabs available.

In the next chapter, we will prepare our application for its release using Android Studio. First, you will learn about the necessary steps to prepare the application before building it in the release mode. You will also learn how applications are compressed in APK files and how to generate your own APK file. Finally, you will learn how to get your certificate as a developer and how to generate a signed APK file, making it ready for release.

9
Preparing for Release

In the previous chapter, you learned enough to test and debug your application. What do you need to do to prepare your application for its release? How can you do this using Android Studio?

This chapter describes the necessary steps to prepare your application for release using Android Studio. First of all, you will learn about **application packages** (**APK**) files—a variation of the JAR files in which Android applications are packed. You will then learn how you need to change your application after fully testing it. Finally, we will sign our APK file, leaving it ready to upload to Google Play.

These are the topics we'll be covering in this chapter:

- APK files
- Build types
- Preparing for release
- Generating a signed APK
- Signing in release mode

Understanding an APK file

Android applications are packed in a file with the .apk extension. These files are just compressed ZIP files, so their content can easily be explored. An APK file usually contains the following:

- `assets/`: This is a folder that contains the asset files of the application. This is the same `assets` folder that exists in our project.
- `META-INF/`: This is a folder that contains our certificates.
- `lib/`: This is a folder that contains compiled code, in case it is needed for a processor.

- `res/`: This is a folder that contains the application resources such as images, strings, and so on.

- `AndroidManifest.xml`: This is the application manifest file.

- `classes.dex`: This is a file that contains the application's compiled code.

- `resources.arsc`: This is a file that contains some precompiled resources, such as binary XML files.

Having the APK file allows the application to be distributed and installed on the Android operating system. Android applications can be distributed as you prefer: through app markets such as Google Play, Amazon App store, or Opera Mobile Store; through your own website; or even via an e-mail to your users. If you choose one of the two last options, take into account that Android, by default, blocks installations from locations other than Google Play. You should inform your users that they need to disable this restriction in their devices to be able to install your application. They have to check the **Unknown sources** option by navigating to **Settings | Security** in their Android devices.

Build types

Applications have to be signed with a private key when they are built. An application can't be installed in a device or even in the emulator if it is not signed. To build our application, there are two types: **debug** and **release**. Both APK versions contain the same folders and compiled files; the difference is in the key used to sign them. Both modes are explained as follows:

- **Debug**: When we ran and tested our application in the previous chapters, we were in debug mode, but we didn't have a key nor did we do anything to sign our application. The Android SDK tools automatically create a debug key, an alias, and their passwords to sign the APK. This process occurs when we are running or debugging our application with Android Studio without us realizing. We can't publish an APK signed with the debug key created by the SDK tools.

- **Release**: When we distribute our application, we have to build a release version. Google Play requires the APK file to be signed with a certificate, for which the developer keeps the private key. In this case, we need our own private key, alias, and password and need to provide them to the build tools. The certificate identifies the developer of the application and can be a self-signed certificate. It is not necessary for a certificate authority to sign the certificate.

Keep the key store with your certificate in a secure place. To upgrade your application, you have to use the same key in order to upload the new version. If you lose the key store, you won't be able to update your application. You will have to create a new application with a different package name.

Steps prior to releasing your app

Before you generate the APK file, it is necessary to prepare your application to build it in release mode. Perform the following steps:

1. Firstly, make sure you have completely tested your application. We recommend testing your application in the following ways:

   ° On a device using the minimum required platform

   ° On a device using the target platform

   ° On a device using the latest available platform

   ° On a real device and not just the emulator

   ° On a variety of screen resolutions and sizes

   ° On a tablet if your application supports it

   ° By switching to landscape mode if you allow it, both in a mobile device and in a tablet

   ° On different network conditions, such as with no Internet connectivity or low coverage

   ° When the GPS or other location service is not activated on your device (if your application uses GPS or any location service)

   ° When the back button is pressed

2. Secondly, we have to check the log messages that are printed from our application. Printing some log messages can be considered a security vulnerability. Logs generated by the Android system can be captured and analyzed, so we should avoid showing critical information about the application's internal working. You should also remove the `android:debuggable` property from the application manifest file. You can also set this property to `false`.

3. Thirdly, if your application communicates with a server, check that the configured URL is the production URL. It is possible that, during the debug phase, you referenced an URL of a server in a prerelease environment.

4. Finally, set the correct value for the `android:versionCode` and `android:versionName` properties from the application manifest file. The version code is a number (integer) that represents the application version. New versions should have greater version codes. This code is used to determine whether an application installed on a device is the latest version or whether there is a newer version.

The version name is a string that represents the application version. Unlike the version code, the version name is visible to the user and appears in the public information about the application. It is just an informative version name to the user and is not used for any internal purpose.

Specify a value of 1 for the version code and 1.0 for the version name. The `manifest` tag should look like the following:

```
<manifest xmlns:android="http://schemas.android.com/apk/res/android"
    package="com.example.myapplication"
    android:versionCode="1"
    android:versionName="1.0" >
```

A new version of our application will have a value of 2 for the version code and could have 1.1 for the version name:

```
<manifest xmlns:android="http://schemas.android.com/apk/res/android"
    package="com.example.myapplication"
    android:versionCode="2"
    android:versionName="1.1" >
```

Generating a signed APK

To generate the signed APK, navigate to **Build | Generate Signed APK**. Select the **app** module and click on the **Next** button. In the dialog to generate the signed APK, we are asked for a certificate. The APK is signed by this certificate, which indicates that it belongs to us.

If this is our first application, we might not have any certificates. Click on the **Create new...** button to open the **New Key Store** dialog. Now, fill in the following information:

- **Key store path**: This is the path in your system to create the key store. The key store is a file with the `.jks` extension, for example, `release_keystore.jks`.

- **Password**: This is the key store password. You have to confirm it.

- **Alias**: This is the alias for your certificate and is a pair of public and private keys. Let's name it `releasekey`.

- **Password**: This is the certificate password. You have to confirm it.
- **Validity (years)**: This is the certificate that will be valid until the validity date. A value of 25 years or more is recommended.
- **Certificate**: This is the personal information contained in the certificate. Type your first and last name, organizational unit, organization, city or locality, state or province, and country code; for example, AS as **Organizational Unit**, packtpub as **Organization**, and ES as **Country Code**.

You can see the **New Key Store** dialog in the next screenshot:

Click on **OK**. The dialog to create the signed APK is now loaded with the key store data. The next time we create a signed APK, we will already have a certificate, so we will select the **Choose existing** button. Click on the **Next** button. In the next step, select the path to save the APK file, select the release build type, and click on **Finish**. When the APK is completely generated, you will be informed by a message on the bottom bar of Android Studio and by the following notification on the top part of Android Studio:

We should have the APK file created in the selected path. Now that you have the APK file ready for release, it is recommended that you test it again in a device before distributing it.

Sign automatically in release mode

Apps are signed automatically when running in debug mode, since the debug key is automatically generated. If we try to run our app in release mode, the following error will be displayed because Android Studio does not know how to sign our app: *Error: The apk for your currently selected variant (app-release-unsigned.apk) is not signed. Please specify a signing configuration for this variant (release).*

We need to configure our build settings if we want to run our app in release mode.

Open the **Project Structure** settings by navigating to **File | Project Structure....** Select your app in the **Modules** section and open the **Signing** tab. Click on the plus button to create a new signing configuration. Rename the configuration and type the data of your key store, as shown in the following screenshot:

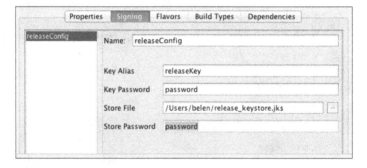

Switch to the **Build Types** tab, in which the default two build types are listed: debug and release. Select **release** and choose the recently created configuration (**releaseConfig**) in the **Signing Config** selector:

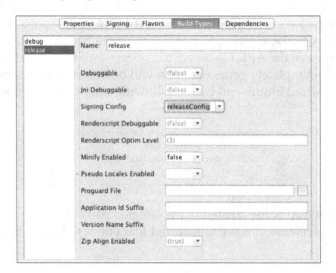

Press **Ok** to finish the configuration. Now, your app will automatically be signed in release mode using your release key.

This signing configuration has actually modified the `build.gradle` file of your app module. Open this file to observe the changes:

- The new signing configuration has been added using the following code:

```
signingConfigs {
    releaseConfig {
        keyAlias 'releaseKey'
        keyPassword 'password'
        storeFile
            file('/Users/belen/release_keystore.jks')
        storePassword 'password'
    }
}
```

- The release build type now points to the previous signing configuration:

```
buildTypes {
    release {
        minifyEnabled false
        proguardFiles
            getDefaultProguardFile('proguard-android.txt'),
            'proguard-rules.pro'
        signingConfig signingConfigs.releaseConfig
    }
}
```

There are some alternatives if you do not want to expose your password in the `build.gradle` file, for example, saving your password in a `properties` file that you can read from the `build.gradle` file.

Running your app in release mode

Now that our app will be signed automatically for release, we can run and test our application using the release mode. To run an app in release mode, open the **Build Variants** panel, which is located in the left-side bar of Android Studio, as you can see in the following screenshot:

Your app module is displayed in the **Build Variants** panel, along with the current build variant, which by default is **debug**. Change the build variant value to **release** and then your app is ready to run in release mode.

APK Analyzer

Android Studio 2.2 introduced a new feature—the **APK Analyzer**. This tool analyzes the content of a selected APK file. You can review the sizes of the components, the final `AndroidManifest.xml` file, and the compiled resources.

Navigate to **Build | APK Analyzer** and select your APK file. A new tab will open with the APK file details, as shown in the next screenshot:

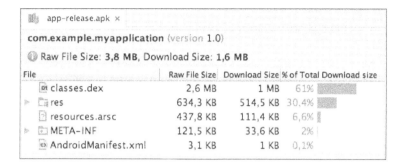

All the files in the APK are listed along with their file sizes: **Raw File Size** and **Download Size**. The download size is the estimation of the file size when the user downloads the APK.

When you select a file, you can see its details in the bottom part. Select the classes. dex file to see the list of all the classes in the APK file, like in the following screenshot:

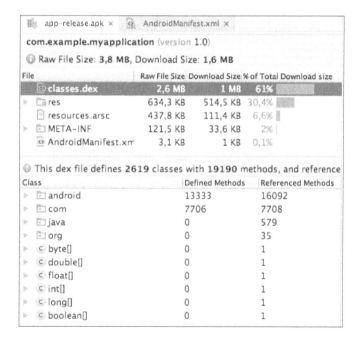

For each class, the number of methods is displayed and a summary is also provided. This information is useful to avoid the 64k referenced method limit issue. There is a limit in the total number of methods that can be referenced within a **Dalvix Executable (dex)** bytecode file: 65536. Using the APK analyzer, you can keep track of the number of methods in your APK.

If your app is over the limit and refactoring or code cleaning are not enough, you can enable a multidex configuration for your app. A multidex configuration will create different dex files. Add the following line in the `defaultConfig` of your `build.gradle` file to enable multidex:

```
multiDexEnabled true
```

You also need to add the `MultiDexApplication` class to your application in the manifest file:

```
android:name="android.support.multidex.MultiDexApplication"
```

Summary

You learned how to make an APK file and how to modify your application to make it ready for release. You also learned how to sign our application using the developer certificate. By the end of this chapter, you should have generated a signed APK prepared for its release.

In *Appendix*, *Getting Help*, you will learn how to get help using Android Studio. We will access the Android Studio online documentation and go through the help topics. Finally, you will learn about keeping your Android Studio instance updated using the inbuilt feature for updates.

Getting Help

While developing applications in a new IDE there will always be doubts about how to perform a certain action. A successful IDE usually includes help wizards and documentation that help users with different problems. Do you wonder how to get help using Android Studio?

In this last chapter we will learn about the Android Studio documentation and help topics. We will learn the topics available in the official documentation which can be accessed online in the official Android website. Finally, we will learn about how to keep our Android Studio instance up-to-date using the update functionality.

The following topics are covered:

- Android Studio help
- Online documentation
- Android Studio updates

Getting help from Android Studio

Android Studio documentation is available in the Android developer website at `https://developer.android.com/studio`. Android Studio documentation is also included in the IntelliJ IDEA web help. This documentation is accessible from Android Studio in the menu **Help | Online Documentation**, or at `http://tools.android.com/welcome-to-android-studio`.

You can navigate to **Help | Help Topics** to directly open the documentation contents tree, or at `http://www.jetbrains.com/idea/webhelp/intellij-idea.html`. There are also some online video tutorials available at `http://tv.jetbrains.net/`.

To quickly find actions of Android Studio, we can use the **Help | Find Action** option. Type the action you are looking for and the list of matching actions will be displayed. You can change some preferences values directly from the list dialog, or you can click to navigate to them. The following screenshot shows the **Find Action** functionality.

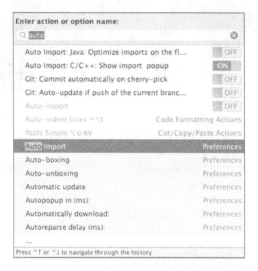

Android Studio provides the tip of the day functionality. The tip of the day explains in a dialog a trick about Android Studio. Every time you open Android Studio, this dialog is shown. We can navigate through more tips using the **Previous Tip** and **Next Tip** buttons. By deselecting the **Show Tips on Startup** checkbox, we can disable this functionality. The tip dialog can be opened by navigating to **Help | Tip of the Day**. The next screen show is an example of a tip of the day screen.

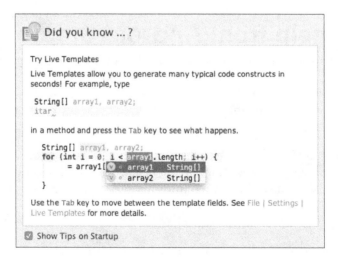

Android online documentation

The official Android documentation provided by Google is available at `http://developer.android.com/`. This documentation contains all the necessary guides to learn not only how to program Android applications, but also how to design for Android and how to distribute and promote our applications. Since this website is quite extensive, here we are listing some of the specific guides useful to increase the knowledge exposed throughout the chapters of this book:

1. *Chapter 1, Installing and Configuring Android Studio*:

    ° Android Studio documentation, at `http://developer.android.com/tools/studio/index.html`

    ° Known issues, at `http://tools.android.com/knownissues`

2. *Chapter 2, Starting a Project*:

    ° App Bar, at `https://developer.android.com/training/appbar/index.html`

    ° Floating action button, at `https://www.google.com/design/spec/components/buttons-floating-action-button.html`

    ° Fragments, at `https://developer.android.com/guide/components/fragments.html`

    ° Navigation drawer, at `https://www.google.com/design/spec/patterns/navigation-drawer.html`

    ° Using code templates, at `https://developer.android.com/studio/projects/templates.html`

3. *Chapter 3, Navigating a Project*:

    ° Manage your project, at `https://developer.android.com/studio/projects/index.html`

    ° App manifest, at `https://developer.android.com/guide/topics/manifest/manifest-intro.html`

4. *Chapter 4, Using the Code Editor*:

    ° Default Keymap reference, at `https://resources.jetbrains.com/assets/products/intellij-idea/IntelliJIDEA_ReferenceCard_mac.pdf`

    ° File and code templates, at `https://www.jetbrains.com/help/idea/2016.1/file-and-code-templates.html`

5. *Chapter 5, Creating User Interfaces:*

    ° Layouts, at `http://developer.android.com/guide/topics/ui/declaring-layout.html`

    ° Input controls, at `http://developer.android.com/guide/topics/ui/controls.html`

    ° Input events, at `http://developer.android.com/guide/topics/ui/ui-events.html`

    ° Supporting multiple screens, at `http://developer.android.com/guide/practices/screens_support.html`

6. *Chapter 6, Tools:*

    ° SDK manager, at `https://developer.android.com/studio/intro/update.html`

    ° Create and manage virtual devices, at `https://developer.android.com/studio/run/managing-avds.html`

    ° Android Emulator, at `https://developer.android.com/studio/run/emulator.html`

    ° Version your app, at `https://developer.android.com/studio/publish/versioning.html`

7. *Chapter 7, Google Play Services:*

    ° Google Play Services, at `https://developers.google.com/android/guides/overview`

8. *Chapter 8, Debugging:*

    ° Using DDMS, at `https://developer.android.com/studio/profile/ddms.html`

    ° Reading and writing logs, at `https://developer.android.com/studio/debug/log.html`

    ° Profiling with Traceview and dmtracedump, at `https://developer.android.com/studio/profile/traceview.html`

    ° About Instant Run, at `https://developer.android.com/studio/run/index.html`

9. *Chapter 9, Preparing for Release:*

    ° Publish your app, at `https://developer.android.com/studio/publish/index.html`

    ° Configure your build, at `https://developer.android.com/studio/build/index.html`

Updates

From the **Help** menu we can check for updates of Android Studio. Navigate to **Help | Check for Update** (**Android Studio | Check for Updates** on Mac). When the checking finishes, if there is an available update of Android Studio we have not installed, the update info is shown in a dialog. This dialog is shown in the following screenshot:

We can look over our current version and the new version code. We can choose if we want to ignore the update (the **Ignore This Update** button), update it later (the **Remind Me Later** button), review the online release notes about the update (the **Release Notes** button), or install the update (the **Download** button). Click on this last option to update Android Studio. The update starts to download first, then Android Studio will restart, and the update will be installed.

If we already have the latest version of Android Studio, the following message will be shown:

You already have the latest version of Android Studio installed.

To configure automatic update settings, see the Updates dialog of your IDE settings

Click on the **Updates** link to open the updates configuration dialog, which is shown in the next screenshot. This dialog provides the current version details, the Android SDK Tools version, the Android Platform version, or the last time we checked for updates. We can select if we want Android Studio to automatically check for updates and what type of updates to check: **Canary Channel**, **Dev Channel**, **Beta Channel**, or **Stable Channel**.

We can examine the information about the recent Android Studio updates by navigating to the menu **Help | What's New in Android Studio**. This information is available online at `http://tools.android.com/recent`. To get the current version we have of Android Studio or even the Java version in our system, navigate to **Help | About (Android Studio | About Android Studio** on Mac).

Summary

We have learned how to use the Android Studio documentation in case we need help with any action available in the IDE. We have also learned about the update feature to always have the latest version of Android Studio installed. By the end of this chapter, the user should be able to search for help using the online documentation and the help topics, and to keep his Android Studio updated with the latest features at his disposal.

Index

R

release mode
  about 136
  APK Analyzer 142-144
  application, executing in 142
  application, signing automatically 140, 141
resources folder
  about 27
  anim/ 27
  color/ 27
  drawable/ 27
  layout/ 27
  menu/ 27
  mipmap/ 27
  values/ 27

S

screen density
  hdpi 59
  ldpi 58
  mdpi 58
  tvdpi 58
  xhdpi 59
  xxhdpi 59
screen size
  extra large 60
  large 60
  normal 60
  small 60
signed APK
  generating 138, 139
Smart Type Completion 39
Software Development Kit Manager
  about 72
  setting up 72-74
System Information tab 130

T

tasks
  managing 88
text-based editor 50
Threads tab
  about 125
  method profiling 125-127

U

UI theme
  modifying 61-64
user interface (UI) 49

V

version control systems (VCS) 89
View object, properties
  android:alpha 56
  android:background 56
  android:clickable 57
  android:elevation 57
  android:fadeScrollbars 57
  android:focusable 57
  android:foreground 57
  android:foregroundTint 57
  android:id 57
  android:minHeight 57
  android:minWidth 57
  android:padding 57
  android:scrollIndicators 57
  android:textAlignment 57
  android:visibility 57
view, types
  Android 24
  Packages 23
  Project 23
  Scopes 24
  Scratches 23

W

warm swap 121